Journalism's Racial Reckoning

T0353028

This book addresses endemic issues of racism in news media at what is a critical moment in time, as journalists around the world speak out en masse against the prejudice and inequality in the industry.

As the events of 2020 – the death of George Floyd, the rise in prominence of the Black Lives Matter movement – have drawn new and focused attention to inequality, white supremacy, and systemic racism, including in the media, this volume chronicles this racial reckoning, revisiting and examining the issues that it has raised. The author analyzes media output by racialized and Indigenous journalists, identifying the racial make-up of newsrooms; the dominance of white perspectives in news coverage; interpretations of ethics downplaying systemic racism and bias; ignorance of racist history in editorial decisions and news content; and diversity and inclusion measures. The actions taken by news organizations in response to the reckoning are also detailed and placed in the context of existing race and media scholarship, to offer emerging strategies to address journalism's longstanding issues with racism in news content and newsrooms.

Grounding the interplay between news media and race within this pivotal moment in history, this text will be an important resource for students and scholars of journalism, journalism ethics, sociology, cultural studies, organizational studies, media and communication studies.

Brad Clark is Associate Professor of Broadcast Media Studies and Journalism at Mount Royal University, Canada.

Routledge Focus on Journalism Studies

For more information about this series, please visit: https://www.
routledge.com

Journalism's Racial Reckoning

The News Media's Pivot to Diversity and Inclusion

Brad Clark

Routledge
Taylor & Francis Group

LONDON AND NEW YORK

First published 2022
by Routledge
4 Park Square, Milton Park, Abingdon, Oxon OX14 4RN

and by Routledge
605 Third Avenue, New York, NY 10158

Routledge is an imprint of the Taylor & Francis Group, an informa business

British Library Cataloguing-in-Publication Data
A catalogue record for this book is available from the British Library

Library of Congress Cataloging-in-Publication Data
Names: Clark, Brad, author.
Title: Journalism's racial reckoning: the news media's pivot to diversity and inclusion/Brad Clark.
Description: London; New York: Routledge, 2022. |
Series: Routledge focus on journalism studies |
Includes bibliographical references and index.
Identifiers: LCCN 2021060370 (print) | LCCN 2021060371 (ebook) |
ISBN 9781032186467 (hardback) | ISBN 9781032199108 (paperback) |
ISBN 9781003261544 (ebook)
Subjects: LCSH: Mass media and minorities. | Mass media and race relations. | Race relations in mass media. | Racism in mass media. | Race discrimination—Press coverage. | Diversity in the workplace.
Classification: LCC P94.5.M55 C53 2022 (print) |
LCC P94.5.M55 (ebook) | DDC 305.8—dc23/eng/20211214
LC record available at https://lccn.loc.gov/2021060370
LC ebook record available at https://lccn.loc.gov/2021060371

ISBN: 978-1-032-18646-7 (hbk)
ISBN: 978-1-032-19910-8 (pbk)
ISBN: 978-1-003-26154-4 (ebk)

DOI: 10.4324/9781003261544

Typeset in Times New Roman
by codeMantra

For my all-time favorite collaborators, Heidi, McKenna, and Bryson.

Contents

Introduction – 2020
"A Year Like No Other" in Journalism Too

It started with the horrifying mobile phone video of a Minneapolis police officer lethally kneeling on the neck of a Black man who pleaded, "I can't breathe!" Protesters took to the streets in Minneapolis the next day, demanding justice for George Floyd, the latest Black person to be killed by law enforcement in the United States. Those demonstrators would soon be joined by people all over the world calling out police brutality and decrying systemic racism. Black Lives Matter (BLM) marches sprang up on virtually every continent, and the movement swelled into a global social justice campaign. Statues of racist leaders and slaveholders were toppled, racist logos and brands were finally eliminated, corporations, universities – in fact, most institutions – were forced to explain their records on race. Journalism was not spared in the calls to account.

The scale of the protests was unprecedented, and pundits started to suggest 2020 was "a year like no other," and the term "racial reckoning" came into popular use to try and describe what was happening. Whether that is an accurate or appropriate term is open to debate, but in the case of journalism, a reckoning was long overdue. Racialized and Indigenous journalists everywhere spoke out on social media, in mainstream news columns and articles, on professional websites, and on the airwaves. They explained the impact of systemic racism in the ways they are treated in their newsrooms, and in the news content that too often neglects their communities or perpetuates tropes of criminality, addiction, dependence, and negativity. Their words and actions drove many of their employers to reconsider the tired diversity and inclusion policies of the past, and to come up with plans for real reform.

That is where the idea for this book originated. As 2020 progressed through the pandemic lockdowns, and I watched the reckoning from my "temporary" home office, the courage of the journalists who called out their employers, and the insights they offered, seemed like a story

DOI: 10.4324/9781003261544-1

that needed to be told. As a journalism and broadcast media educator in an era when the field has never faced more threats, it seemed to me that there was so much to learn through the actions and responses of news staff and news organizations.

My perspective on issues of diversity, equity, and inclusion is one that comes from the deepest privilege. I am a white, cisgendered, heterosexual, settler male living in the Treaty 7 territory of the Niitsitapi (Blackfoot), Tsuut'ina, the Îyârhe Nakoda, and the Metis Nation in what has come to be known as southern Alberta. There are clear biases that come with such positionality. In writing about the experiences of Indigenous and racialized journalists, I seek to represent their views authentically, and not speak on their behalf, nor to suggest that I am more qualified than anyone else to do this work. While this book is meant to de-center whiteness by focusing on the perspectives of Black, racialized, and Indigenous news workers, it is worth noting that much of the classic scholarship in this area itself emerged from the white, patriarchal, colonial pursuit of academic research. Of course, those same forces explain why better representation in the news discourse has been a constant struggle.

This book sets out to capture the racial reckoning in journalism and to identify emerging, effective strategies to build a more equitable, authentic, and accurate news production system in mainstream media. Racial justice drove much of the debate and discussion through 2020; so much of the research and analysis here focuses on that particular line of difference. This is not to suggest that news media are not responsible to better represent gender, LGTBQ2S+ groups, or people with disabilities. In many cases, news organizations included these groups in their diversity and inclusion strategies, but the scope of the analysis for much of this volume is driven by the words and deeds of Indigenous and racialized news workers through this period.

The first chapter starts with the chronology of Black people killed by police in the United States, the response of the communities, and the broader racial reckoning brought to bear on all institutions, including news media. It covers the timeline of mainstream news organizations in the United States, Canada, the United Kingdom, and Australia as they stumbled from one controversy to another over coverage that was too often sensational and stereotypic. As BLM gained momentum, so too did the apparent willingness of racialized and Indigenous journalists to call out their employers. The interplay between journalists and their managers over longstanding but ongoing issues of systemic racism in journalism is detailed.

Chapter 2 is an analysis of the opinions, experiences, and frustrations of Black, Indigenous, and people of color working in news media shared in scores of media accounts aggregated over the course of 2020. These journalists highlighted contradictions in journalism's long-held ethical codes, a toxic environment in many mainstream newsrooms, and the failure of diversity initiatives to address systemic racism in news content and the workplace. The analysis supports existing research on diversity and inclusion in journalism, that journalistic practice and ethics are deeply entrenched in white supremacy.

The third chapter takes the findings from Chapter 2 and places them in the context of all the previous scholarship examining journalism and race, adding further corroboration and theoretical clarity to the observations of racialized news media workers. Two cases from the racial reckoning are presented to draw the connection between the existing body of research on race and journalistic practice and the current newsgathering environment. One looks at the experiences of a Black photojournalist covering BLM protests in New York and his approach to taking more authentic pictures. The other discusses coverage of the Mi'kmaw lobster fishery on Canada's Atlantic coast, and issues of false balance and missing historical context in the mainstream narrative.

Chapter 4 similarly builds on the findings of the Chapter 2 analysis, comparing the earlier findings with 50 years of diversity measures and their limited effectiveness, looking at participation rates for Indigenous and racialized journalists, the challenges they continue to face in largely white newsrooms, and why diversity so often remains elusive. The focus on simply hiring diverse news staff, without addressing the frustrations and concerns raised by racialized and Indigenous journalists through the racial reckoning, explains issues with retention, and the limited progress toward more representative newsrooms.

Chapter 5 shifts the focus from the workers to the managers and news organizations, analyzing and categorizing their responses to the reckoning. The scope of responses was quite wide, ranging from no actions at all to real steps to deal with the concerns of racialized staff. The range of initiatives undertaken by mainstream news organizations is described, with an emphasis on some of the most innovative, especially those focused on accountability and transparency.

The final chapter concludes with an overview of the best strategies from the racial reckoning and how they can be deployed to mitigate systemic racism in news content and the workplace. Supports for racialized and Indigenous news workers are augmented with additional measures to create space for under-represented voices, to establish an ethical position beyond the moral muteness associated with orthodox objectivity, to prioritize diversity in supervisory and management roles, and to hold news organizations to account with their staff and audiences. Examples of how these approaches are already working are described. The book ends with an epilogue of the racial reckoning, the pushback against the anti-racism movement and its proponents, and the conclusion that 2020 was just one step in a long journey to equality.

1 The Racial Reckoning in Journalism

Introduction

The murder of George Floyd under the knee of a Minneapolis police officer in May 2020 launched a wave of protest initially aimed at law enforcement, but grew into a broad-based stand against systemic racism in all segments of Western society. As Black Lives Matter (BLM) demonstrators took to the streets across the United States, Canada, the United Kingdom, Australia, Europe, and parts of Africa, journalists of color began to speak out en masse about their experiences of racism in their own organizations and industry. This was driven by frequently stereotypic, one-sided, sensational coverage of police violence and the BLM movement, coverage that drew the condemnation of racialized and Indigenous journalists and their allies in their newsrooms. This chapter chronicles the manifold missteps of mainstream news organizations through the racial reckoning, particularly in the United States and Canada, detailing a string of controversies at *The New York Times*, The Canadian Broadcasting Corporation, Global News, *The Washington Post*, *The Philadelphia Inquirer*, *The Toronto Star*, and other news organizations. The unprecedented, ensuing backlash led to resignations, suspensions, job action, apologies, and promises of reform. In Australia and the United Kingdom, there were also editorial conflicts over BLM protest coverage at ABC, SBS, the BBC, and *The Age*, precipitating debates on the overwhelming whiteness of news staff and its impact on newsroom dynamics and the coverage of racial issues. However, in North America there was generally a much more sustained outpouring of profound critique, analysis, and insight from Indigenous and racialized news media workers in the form of op-eds, columns, personal essays, social media posts, and other published media accounts. That outpouring undoubtedly shaped the discussion in other parts of the world. Despite the varying

DOI: 10.4324/9781003261544-2

regional demographics, the impact of systemic racism in journalism is similarly felt in the countries considered here. This chapter captures the racial reckoning in journalism through 2020, describing the conditions and events that sparked a global movement, the response of news media, and the fallout from that response on an industry already in peril on so many fronts.

Police Killings, the Pandemic, and Systemic Racism

The image of a Minneapolis police officer kneeling on the neck of George Floyd, a Black man, gasping the familiar refrain "I can't breathe!" before dying on the road, was the just latest in a long history of deadly excess at the hands of white police officers and vigilantes in the United States. Through the first five months of 2020, the names Ahmaud Arbery, Breonna Taylor, and Rayshard Brooks preceded Floyd, and before them Elijah McClain, Philando Castile, Eric Garner, Freddie Gray, Trayvon Martin, and many more. At around the same time in Canada, police killings of Chantal Moore, a Tla-o-qui-aht First Nation woman, in New Brunswick, and Pakistani immigrant Ejaz Ahmed Choudry in Toronto, similarly drew attention to the high rates of death in interactions between law enforcement and racialized and Indigenous Peoples. Despite its terrible familiarity, somehow the video footage of Floyd's cruel death galvanized anger on a mass scale, bringing millions of protesters to the streets, first in the United States, but then in Canada and around the world.

The protesters' anger was supported by ample data. The discriminatory application of justice in Western colonial democracies is longstanding and well-documented. The difference in the 21st century seems to be that mobile phone video of the excesses of law enforcement against racialized and Indigenous Peoples has become a common feature of social media. The footage shared on Twitter, Facebook, and Instagram confirms the overwhelming statistical evidence of systemic racism in policing and the courts. Studies in the United States show a higher "lifetime risk" of being killed by police for African Americans, Native Americans, and LatinX men compared to white people (Edwards, Hedwig, & Esposito, 2019). The risk is highest for Black men, who are 2.5 times more likely to be killed by police than white men. There are more Black people in US prisons than any other racial group even though they make up only 12 per cent of the population. The rate of imprisonment for Black adults is almost six times the rate for whites, while Hispanics are imprisoned at three times the white rate (Gramlich, 2019).

The numbers are similar north of the border. The John Howard Society of Canada states that Black and Indigenous Peoples are significantly overrepresented in prisons, "by more than 300 per cent versus their population" for Blacks, while for First Nations, Métis, and Inuit peoples "the over representation is nearly 500 per cent," and "these imbalances are getting worse, not better" (John Howard Society, 2017). When it comes to police killings, again, "Indigenous and Black people are overwhelmingly overrepresented," for example, an analysis of data from 2007 to 2017 concludes "Indigenous peoples represented one third of people shot to death by RCMP [Royal Canadian Mounted Police]" despite making up just six per cent of the population, while another report determined "a Black person was more than 20 times more likely to be shot and killed by the police compared to a white person" (Ontario Human Rights Commission, 2018, cited in Stelkia, 2020).

Despite the quick assertions by many white politicians responding to BLM protests that racism is not a problem in the United Kingdom, statistics show an overrepresentation of Blacks and ethnic minorities in British prisons as well; "Black people comprise 3 per cent of the overall population in England and Wales, [while] they currently make up 12 per cent of its prison population" (Koram, 2020). In fact, "we're locking more of our Black people away than the big, bad USA." In Australia, Indigenous rates of incarceration are even higher than those for Black people in the United States, making up "slightly more than 3 per cent of the Australian population but comprise 28 per cent of the adult prison population and over 50 per cent of juvenile detainees" (Cunneen, 2020). The death rate of Indigenous inmates in Australia has been so pervasive that a royal commission was struck to investigate in 1987.

The systemic racism borne out of these statistics was also revealed in the apparent double standard in the treatment of white people accused of violence compared to their racialized counterparts. At the height of protests in the United States, Jacob Blake, a Black man in Kenosha, Wisconsin, was shot in the back by police after a domestic dispute and survived. However, in the ensuing BLM protests, a white teenager, Kyle Rittenhouse, was accused of killing two protesters, and wounding a third. When Rittenhouse was granted bail, and not held in custody pending trial, it drew criticism from social justice advocates, who wondered if a person of color accused of double homicide would ever receive such compassion. At the end of a controversial trial in November 2021, Rittenhouse was found not guilty on all charges. While officers involved in George Floyd's murder were charged, and

Derek Chauvin was eventually found guilty of murder, only one police official involved in Breonna Taylor's death was ever indicted and only on relatively minor charges.

The day after George Floyd's murder in late May, angry citizens took to the streets in Minneapolis, the first of many protests. A day later BLM marches took place across the country, and by early July BLM had become what *The New York Times* described as "the largest movement in the country's history" (Buchanan, Bui, & Patel, 2020). Within days of Floyd's death, there were rallies, marches, and protests in every Canadian province and territory. Thousands turned out for demonstrations in major cities in Europe, Africa, and Asia. Most were peaceful but in some cases statues of prominent colonial leaders and individuals associated with the slave trade were toppled or defaced. It was not long before demonstrations against racial injustice at the hands of law enforcement evolved into something more: a broad reckoning over racism past and present.

The Resurgence of Black Lives Matter

BLM was founded in 2013, originally as a hashtag, after the acquittal of the man who killed Trayvon Martin in Sanford, Florida. The organization's website states that:

> Black Lives Matter Global Network Foundation, Inc. is a global organization in the US, UK, and Canada, whose mission is to eradicate white supremacy and build local power to intervene in violence inflicted on Black communities by the state and vigilantes.
>
> Black Lives Matter (2021)

The network is described as a "decentralized, grassroots movement" that seeks to support Black people and challenge racial discrimination, particularly in the justice system (Leazenby & Polk, 2020). In addition to the global network there are local chapters.

However, after the murder of George Floyd, support for BLM and antiracism initiatives reached levels never seen before. In addition to demonstrations around the world, donations to BLM and other groups took off. According to Candid, which tracks global philanthropy, "roughly $5 billion in pledges and commitments were made to racial equity organisations" between May 25 and the end of July (Murphy, 2020). What started out as protests against anti-Black police brutality grew into a movement much wider in scope, touching virtually every aspect of society. Corporations sought to address their own complicity in racism by donating to social justice causes and charities.

In addition to writing cheques, there were prominent actions taken to address longstanding racist history. While protesters removed monuments of racist leaders or slave owners in the United Kingdom, the United States, and Canada, governments and public institutions also took down such artifacts and began renaming places commemorating figures with a racist past. Companies and universities were called out for poor records on diversity, despite promises to the contrary, and issued statements promising to be more inclusive and to fight systemic racism. Brands featuring stereotypic namesakes – Aunt Jemima and Uncle Ben's – were finally dropped after years of criticism. In the world of sport, players in European soccer leagues wore BLM slogans and knelt in solidarity before games, emulating Colin Kaepernick, the Black, former quarterback who was blacklisted for that exact form of protest by the National Football League only a few years ago. The Canadian Football League's Edmonton franchise dropped the nickname Eskimos, a term offensive to Inuit, and the Washington Football Team played its first NFL season after dropping the derogatory Redskins from its mantle after years of pressure. Every North American sports league rolled out antiracism campaigns of one kind or another. The Women's National Basketball Association dedicated its season to the memory of Breonna Taylor. The broader, society-wide movement for racial justice came to be known as "the racial reckoning," and virtually every institution was forced to consider its own culpability in systemic racism. In the United States, job postings for diversity officers surged (McGregor, 2020). Equity legislation and measures were adapted in many government jurisdictions in the United States and beyond.

The United States, pushed by the BLM movement after the death of George Floyd, became the epicenter for global action on racial justice. The lethal excesses of law enforcement had been highlighted by viral social media video in the past, but Floyd's murder was different, as one activist told the BBC, "it was a completely unambiguous act of injustice – where people could see this man [Floyd] was completely unarmed and incapacitated" (Cheung, 2020b). The pandemic had undoubtedly further heightened awareness of systemic racism as racialized, Black, and Indigenous Peoples experienced disproportionally higher infection and death rates, and more unemployment (Chavez, 2020). People of Asian descent were blamed for the virus and targeted in racist attacks. US president Donald Trump's anti-immigrant and anti-Muslim policies, in addition to his defense of white supremacists, attacks on racialized Democrats who are women, and blanket condemnation of BLM protesters, further inspired the movement. Observers described the moment as a "tipping point," a "perfect storm for rebellion" and "the last straw" (Ellis, 2020; Cheung, 2020a). The impact was visually represented on streets where "Black Lives Matter" was painted in giant block letters (including in front of the White House), in banners and slogans in sports arenas and stadiums, in the updated packaging seen on the shelves of grocery stores, and likely at the polls in US elections in November.

Consumers of news also watched as mainstream newspapers, television, and radio networks and digital media were also forced to consider their role in maintaining systemic racism in their newsrooms and content. As the next section demonstrates, many of the best known and established news media organizations in the Western world were swept up in a racial reckoning of their own, largely driven by the racialized, Black, and Indigenous journalists they employ. Often it was the news media's own ham-handed coverage that triggered criticism.

Familiar Patterns of White-Led News Coverage and Racism

The BLM demonstrations continued through much of the summer in some cities, despite challenges associated with the pandemic. The news media had much to cover: the longstanding issue of racism and police brutality, the interaction between law enforcement and protesters, calls to defund the police, and efforts to remove monuments and placenames of Confederate leaders, slaveholders, and known racists. The disproportionately high impact of COVID-19 on marginalized groups, and racist attacks on East Asians, further fueled demands for racial justice, and added to the news agenda. News media were suddenly forced to consider systemic racism on a scale never seen before. As they grappled with all the issues of the moment, they were also sending reporters into the streets, and in a few cases, journalists were attacked by rioters and riot police. A Black reporter for CNN was arrested on live television in Minneapolis (and released soon after), while a white colleague nearby was allowed to continue his work (*The Guardian*, 2020). While there were some instances of rioting and looting, one analysis showed that "about 93 per cent of the racial-justice protests that swept the United States…remained peaceful and non-destructive" (Craig, 2020). Nonetheless, the political discourse – captured by President Trump's threat on Twitter, "when the looting starts the shooting starts" – focused on protester violence and dominated much of the reporting. The coverage and the commentary carried by mainstream news organizations drew heavy criticism from both outside and inside newsrooms, and the media's complicity in systemic racism became part of the broader discussion.

As the focal point for the racial reckoning, the United States was home to the most extensive discourse related to race and news production; however, Canadian news media were similarly forced to consider their own historic record. Though the level of discussion was not as high in the United Kingdom or Australia, racialized journalists in those countries also called out inequity and discrimination in their organizations. The news media's handling of the reckoning, especially as it related to their own industry, is detailed nation-by-nation below.

The United States

The preeminent *New York Times* became a hub for the racial reckoning and journalism, on the pages of its opinion section and in the social media posts of news staff. The initial feud between journalists and management was triggered when an editorial by Arkansas Republican Senator Tom Cotton was published calling for military intervention against BLM protests under the headline "Send in the Troops" (Cotton, 2020). Without referencing any of the underlying issues of the discrimination driving protests, Cotton steered into unsubstantiated conspiracy theories writing "cadres of left-wing radicals like antifa [are] infiltrating protest marches to exploit Floyd's death for their own anarchic purposes." The column was met with condemnation by news workers associated with a Slack group, Black@NYT. In addition to challenging the veracity of Cotton's assertions, they pointed out the violence inherent in his call for military intervention, that such a threat to unarmed civilians exercising their constitutional rights put the lives of Black journalists in peril (McBain, 2020). Within hours of its posting, *Times* staff were tweeting a screen shot of the column with the caption "Running this puts Black @nytimes staff in danger" while management defended the editorial, at first (Smith, 2020). The discussion on social media broadened from Cotton to racism and its impact on news and newsrooms. Brent Staples, a journalist, wrote on Twitter that Black staff drew suspicion from supervisors for "split loyalties," and when he was critical of reporting at a newspaper early in his career a manager told him "'we worry that you are here pushing a black agenda'...In other words, I was welcome to stay – only if I subscribed to what critical race theorists would later describe as the 'white normative view' of world events" (Staples, 2020). *Times* employees sent a letter with about 1,000 signatures to publisher A. G. Sulzberger condemning the Cotton essay as "an affront to our standards for ethical and accurate reporting" (Smith, 2020). *Times* management reversed its position on the column, added a long editor's note describing all the failings of the newspaper in publishing the piece, and the opinion section editor, James Bennet, resigned. Ben Smith reported on the episode on the page of the *Times*, suggesting a reckoning was only getting started, and that "staff members are pressing for changes beyond the Opinion section" (Smith, 2020).

A few weeks later the *Times* published an opinion piece by Wesley Lowery, the Pulitzer Prize winning journalist who left *The Washington Post* over clashes related to social media and racial justice coverage with managing editor Marty Baron. In his essay, Lowery used the controversies at the *Times* and other mainstream news media as a foundation to discredit notions of "professed objectivity" pointing out that "objective truth" is determined "almost exclusively by white reporters and their mostly white bosses" all with a view to "avoid offending the sensibilities of white readers" (Lowery, 2020). A reckoning, he suggested, was overdue:

> The turmoil at The Times and the simultaneous eruptions inside other newsrooms across the country are the predictable results of the mainstream media's labored refusal to racially integrate. It has been more than 50 years since the first black journalists appeared in mainstream American newsrooms. For all of that time, black journalists have made meager demands: Please hire some more of us. Please pay us the way you do our colleagues. Please allow us to ascend to leadership roles. Please consider our opinions about how accurate and fair coverage of all communities, especially our own, can be achieved.
>
> Lowery (2020)

At the *Los Angeles Times*, an organization ostensibly serving one of the most diverse communities in the United States, concerns over racial inequality in the newsroom and coverage of BLM protests boiled over into what was described as an "internal uprising" (Folkenflik, 2020). Through the first few days of national protests, when there was growing support across all social media platforms for BLM, an email was sent to *L.A. Times* interns warning "If you're unable or unwilling to follow the [*L.A. Times'* social media] guidelines below, I respect that and we can arrange for your last day a bit sooner than originally planned" (Wagner & Strachan, 2020). Around the same time, there was deep concern over the news coverage of BLM demonstrations exemplified in a story headlined, "Looters who hit L.A. stores explain what they did: 'Get my portion!'" News staff responded with outrage in a "multi-day conversation in the company's #diversity Slack channel around the company's coverage of the protests" and urged the *L.A. Times* to "publicly take a firm anti-racism editorial position and privately work to address its racial inequities" (Wagner & Strachan, 2020). Other journalists, such as Esmerelda Bermudez, highlighted years of frustration with management in seeking a more diverse newsroom, while Blacks and Latinos remained under-represented. In what would become a familiar pattern, management acknowledged its mistakes, senior editors resigned, and there were promises to do better. A class-action lawsuit brought by journalists of color seeking pay equity with white colleagues was settled. Black and Latino caucuses of the *L.A. Times'* union called for hiring, promotion and support of racialized workers, "a profound reorientation of our coverage around communities of color," and for an apology related to the decades of racist coverage, specifically the "fomenting episodes of anti-Latino hysteria in California and the United States" (Chan, 2020). In the last Sunday edition in September, the *L.A. Times* published "Our reckoning with racism" a 3,300-word editorial detailing the newspaper's historic role in maintaining white supremacy, supporting the internment of Japanese Americans, stereotyping Latinos and Blacks, and backing anti-immigrant political candidates.

The *Philadelphia Inquirer* triggered outrage for an editorial on its pages titled "Buildings Matter, Too," a crass rebuke to BLM. Forty-four workers at the paper called in "sick and tired" in protest. They sent a letter to management explaining their actions, stating "we're tired of seeing our words and photos twisted to fit a narrative that does not reflect our reality. We're tired of being told to show both sides of issues there are no two sides of" (McBain, 2020). A senior editor responsible for the piece resigned.

News staff and the executive editor at the *Pittsburgh Post-Gazette* were also locked in a standoff after Alexis Johnson, one of the publication's few Black journalists, was pulled off protest coverage over a tweet the editor felt showed bias (Humphries, 2020). Johnson was responding to complaints by some people that BLM protests in Pittsburgh had left garbage and debris, tweeting photos of a similar mess from a country music event, with the text, "Horrifying scenes and aftermath from selfish LOOTERS who don't care about this city!!!!!... oh wait sorry. No, these are pictures from a Kenny Chesney concert tailgate. Whoops" (Johnson, 2020). Other reporters who spoke out in support of Johnson were also banned. A white male reporter who had posted tweets about BLM protests was only given a warning (Romine, 2020). The union representing news staff issued a statement citing concerns about the treatment of Johnson, as well as editorial decisions taken by the paper to heavily edit stories about the demonstrations.

At *The Washington Post*, news staff unrest led to a town hall, described as "tense," in which editor Marty Baron apologized for failing "to address 'the particular and severe burden felt by black employees, many of whom were also covering the story' of the protests" (Smith, 2020). *The Post*'s union responded with an email and petition to staff noting that the "voices the company chose to elevate in this moment belonged exclusively to white people. There could be no starker example of The Post's lack of diversity in management." *Post* Publisher Fred Ryan responded in an email of his own, stating that the newspaper had long worked to improve diversity, but that "we also know there is more to be done – and we are committed to doing it" (Farhi & Ellison, 2020). Less than a week later *The Post* announced it was adding a dozen new positions aimed at improving coverage of race, including a senior role titled "managing editor for diversity and inclusion" (WashPostPR, 2020).

Most of the biggest names in media were also swept up in reckonings related to the wider racial justice movement, often with more resignations, promises to "do better," and announcements of new initiatives coordinated by their public relations departments. ABC News was forced to put executive Barbara Fedida on leave related to a "history of insensitive comments" including a reference to Black *Good Morning America* anchor Robin Roberts, and "picking cotton" (Ali, 2020). The editor-in-chief of *Variety* was placed on administrative leave after a social media feud over diversity; the top editor at online women's lifestyle publication *Refinery29*, owned by Vice Media, also resigned after former employees of color described a toxic work environment and discrimination; The editor of food magazine *Bon Appetit* was accused of underpaying racialized journalists and resigned after a photo of him in brownface was made public; Ana Wintour, *Vogue*'s longtime editor-in-chief, issued an apology for her publication's failure to promote racialized writers and designers and for publishing "hurtful and intolerant" content while predictably promising reform as well. Whether called out by their own workers or not, most news organizations across the United States announced steps to boost diversity and inclusion in their newsrooms, and provide deeper, more representative coverage, including Gannett, *The Wall Street Journal*, National Public Radio (NPR), and Bloomberg.

Canada

Media outlets are not nearly as numerous in Canada, given its smaller population; however, the racial reckoning swept through Canadian news organizations as well, with similar force, and similar outcomes. The Canadian Broadcasting Corporation (CBC), the country's public broadcaster, faced a barrage of high-profile controversies related to Indigenous and racialized staff, frequently because of its coverage of BLM. In what was described as an "editorial discussion" about covering issues of racism, one of CBC's most prominent journalists, Wendy Mesley, used "the N-word" and was subsequently suspended (Newman-Bremang, 2020). Imani Walker, an associate producer who was on the call, pointed out on Twitter that Mesley had used the slur previously in front of racialized staff (CBC News, 2020a).

The CBC was called out publicly and internally for coverage of an incident between two New York police cruisers and protesters, describing the episode as a "standoff," and editing out footage of the police cars plowing into the crowd (Goldsbie, 2020a). CBC admitted that the report was misleading and updated the story. It also acknowledged it made a mistake when BLM Toronto co-founder Sandy Hudson was invited to do a radio segment and was then "unbooked" after she raised the issue of defunding the police during her pre-interview, an idea the producer scoffed at (Hudson, 2020). Even when CBC president Catherine Tait issued an internal statement, "Our Stand in Solidarity," to show support for Black, racialized and Indigenous staff, it drew condemnation and critical comments on the CBC's internal website, including this post: "This is an extraordinarily embarrassing and empty response from the leader of a corporation that has grossly mishandled coverage of this crisis and has been complicit in upholding systemic anti-Black racism in this country for a very long time" (Canadaland, 2020).

Indigenous and racialized journalists frankly described their experiences at CBC on social media. In one Twitter thread an Asian journalist, who posted about being repeatedly referred to by the name of another Asian anchor by a former executive, received an apology from that person, but the posted apology used the wrong name *again*. In response, Adrian Cheung (*not* Andrew Chang) wrote, "How do you flunk the test when I literally gave you the answers? I am done with this conversation," (Cheung, 2020a). On Facebook, Christine Genier, the host of *Yukon Morning* and a Ta'an Kwäch'än citizen, shared her frustrations as an Indigenous journalist, including the time a "non-Indigenous colleague showed up at her house uninvited, to explain that the increase in Indigenous reporters in newsrooms had been difficult – for them [the white staff]" (Balkissoon, 2020). Genier resigned from the CBC.

As with their competing news colleagues at CBC, Global News workers were alarmed by their networks' coverage of BLM protests, and in particular an online story about Canadian expats in the United States, a piece that featured no Black sources (Krishnan, 2020). Twelve staff members sent an email to management complaining that the story "frankly perpetuates racism while exacerbating false narratives about what these protests are actually about in the U.S. and Canada." Six of those twelve were laid off weeks later, and a seventh quit (Krishnan, 2020). There were also broader concerns for journalists – the use of insensitive language, instructions from senior editors to sanitize coverage of racial issues – and later in the summer, over 150 past and present employees sent a letter to Global's parent company, Corus Entertainment, "calling out systemic racism" within the company. When the Canadian Association of Black Journalists posted an open letter describing "the negative experiences of Black Corus employees" and urging reform, the president and chief executive of Corus Entertainment, Douglas Murphy, responded that Corus had hired a diversity consultant to investigate, and would wait for a report before commenting on any matter related to diversity and inclusion. A regional news director stepped down from Global News a day after an investigative piece on the company was published by VICE News.

When *National Post* columnist Rex Murphy wrote an editorial titled "Canada is not a racist country, despite what the Liberals say," Postmedia journalists strongly objected to the piece. A note to the online version of the story was later added apologizing for "a failure in the normal editing oversight" and directs readers to a withering op-ed in response from *Post* journalist Vanmala Subramaniam, who characterized Murphy's views on race as "deeply ignorant" (Subramaniam, 2020). However, Murphy was allowed to defend his original column in a subsequent article, and then Conrad Black, the *Post*'s founder, wrote two pieces denying systemic racism describing the reckoning as an "official obsession" (Szklarski, 2020). Some *Post* journalists began to withhold bylines, but management defended the rights of Murphy and Black to share their opinions, while new diversity measures were also being introduced at the company.

The *Toronto Star* published a number of articles, op-eds, and features related to race and news coverage, some of it critical of its own track record. However, complaints came in after an editorial on police violence seemed to "pit Black people against Indigenous people" (Hudson, 2020). When the publication announced to staff that it had appointed Shree Paradkar, a race and gender columnist, to a new internal ombud position to address issues of discrimination and bias in the newsroom, one of its long-serving columnists, Rosie DiManno, sent out her own reply-all email calling the move "a fucking abomination and I will not submit to yet another level of interference in an insanely over-micro-managed newsroom" (Goldsbie, 2020b). While management issued its own note in support of the position soon after, there appeared to be no other action taken against DiManno, who had previously run into trouble for racist language including use of the N-word. The apparent lack of a reprimand drove 62 *Star* employees to sign a letter to management describing DiManno's missive as "an unacceptable denigration of the concerns and experiences of BIPOC [Black, Indigenous, People of Color] newsroom members...an example of the kind of racism, institutional and otherwise, that prompted the need for Paradkar's position" (Goldsbie, 2020b).

Black, racialized, and Indigenous journalists turned to social media to draw attention to the failing of news media at their organizations and others. Twitter hosted a lengthy exchange over a news conference featuring the Toronto Raptors president, Masai Ujiri, a Black man who only a year earlier had been assaulted by a sheriff's deputy as he tried to join his team on the court moments after it had won the National Basketball Association championship. The police official claimed Ujiri did not show his credentials and had assaulted him; however, video of the incident showed that this was patently false. Nonetheless, with NBA players and management firmly backing BLM, *Toronto Sun* reporter Steve Simmons asked Ujiri a question about high rates of gun violence and deaths in Toronto, perceived my many as a coded reference for Black-on-Black crime. Ujiri politely answered, but TSN's Kayla Grey, the first Black woman to host a national sportscast in Canada, quickly followed up by asking "as a Black man" how frustrating it was for Ujiri to get that kind of question (NBA.com, 2020). Sportsnet journalist Donnovan Bennett wrote about the exchange on the network's website, observing that Simmons had basically

> ...asked a man who was a victim of systemic racism if the Toronto Raptors should devote less energy to combating systematic racism. It wasn't a BIPOC journalist who asked this question, but as always, we have to come in and clean up the mess afterward.
>
> Bennett (2020)

By September 2020, as the focus of the BLM movement shifted to elections in the United States, attention to racial justice and the media dissipated somewhat in Canada, until news coverage of Indigenous treaty rights and the Atlantic lobster fishery became an issue. Mobs of non-Indigenous fishermen harassed Mi'kmaw lobster crews on the water and on land, and even set fire to a lobster pound containing the Mi'kmaw's catch. The Mi'kmaq were engaged in a "moderate livelihood" lobster fishery outside the non-Indigenous season as guaranteed by treaty and legal precedent established by the Supreme Court of Canada two decades earlier. Non-Indigenous fisherman claimed the Mi'kmaw harvest would ruin the lobster stock. However, reporting on the issue suggested the Mi'kmaw's actions were illegal (out of season), that their rights were in question, or that they were engaged in a dispute. Indigenous reporters in particular set the record straight on social media and in interviews. Video journalist Trina Roache, a member of the Glooscap First Nation in unceded Mi'kmaw territory, talked to CBC and Canadaland, urging mainstream reporters to learn and understand historical context and the significance of treaty law in covering the story:

> To be dismissive or refer to it as an illegal fishery is really covering over all this backstory and history and this treaty relationship that's very important and really matters today. The treaties might have been signed before but they still count today, and if we're going to report on these stories then we really need to understand what it means.
>
> CBC News (2020b)

Most major Canadian media companies were drawn into the racial justice movement and held to account by news staff for the lack of commitment to diversity and inclusion, as well as for problematic coverage, if not in the moment, then in the past. Denise Balkissoon (2020) shared her experiences over the years as a racialized journalist who grew weary of having to explain her employers' "racially inept stories while out in the world" leaving the *Globe and Mail*, when she became "convinced that no one with real power there was ever going to pursue true equity, either inside the newsroom or in its coverage." Just before Balkissoon's article the union representing the *Globe*'s news staff issued a statement calling out inadequate diversity measures and white privilege at the newspaper. A representative of the Canadian Journalists of Colour, Anita Li, acknowledged that despite some missteps most news organizations had committed to reforms, notably with pressure from their unions: The *Globe*, the *Toronto Star*, Global News, and *The Walrus* (Szklarski, 2020). How far news organizations are willing to go, and what measures they have actually undertaken, are discussed in Chapter 5.

Outside North America: The United Kingdom and Australia

While the United States was undoubtedly the headwaters for the BLM tide, the video of George Floyd's death generated outrage and protest worldwide. Though the frequency and intensity of demonstrations in the United Kingdom and Australia and might not have been as high as in North America, rallies were held in most major cities and drew thousands of protesters. Systemic racism was thrust into the spotlight, statues toppled, and statements of solidarity were issued. A Pew Research Center study found legislators outside the United States referenced the movement on their Twitter accounts in the ten days after Floyd's killing, including 59 per cent of British members of Parliament, and 26 per cent of Australian MPs (Devlin et al., 2020). As in North America, news media became the focus of the racial reckoning, targeted for disproportionately white newsrooms, poor coverage of BLM protests, and complicity in maintaining systemic racism historically.

In the United Kingdom, the BBC drew considerable heat. As the movement gathered momentum, the public broadcaster warned staff not to support BLM in any way, on social media or by attending protests, though it also asserted "the BBC is not neutral on racism" (O'Toole, 2020). However, a *HuffPost* UK investigation found dozens of BBC journalists of color experienced "institutional racism," bullying, and a "colonial" approach in some of its news operations (White, 2020a). They pointed to a persistent lack of racialized staff, despite the urgent calls to boost diversity almost 20 years after Greg Dyke, the then director-general of the BBC, described the corporation as "hideously white." That perception was further supported when the BBC defended the use of the N-word by a journalist quoting racist thugs who attacked a young Black man, saying it was "editorially justified" (White, 2020b). Almost 20,000 complaints were registered, and a Black BBC presenter resigned in disgust over the incident. At the same time, according to government data, "the BBC has been steadily haemorrhaging Black, Asian and minority ethnic (BAME) talent. The number of BAME staff leaving the BBC jumped from 173 in 2014 to 379 a year later, an increase of 120 per cent" (White, 2020a). The BBC program *Newsnight* was denounced for its lack of diversity when it failed to include a single non-white guest on its show during a week in July, according to a study conducted by the group Women in Journalism (Waterson, 2020). The analysis looked at the gender and ethnicity of journalists and sources in print and broadcast media. Across all media lines it found a "shocking lack of diversity" and an over-representation of white men in every metric, even as BLM and the racial reckoning were driving the news agenda (Women in Journalism, 2020). For example, only three out of 111 sources in front-page news stories were minority women, and only about 12 per cent of television reporters were non-white. Black, Asian and minority ethnic journalists spoke out against the systemic racism captured in that study whether it was in internal Zoom calls at the BBC, on social media, or in a letter to the Society of Editors from 50 racialized journalists working at the UK's leading news outlets (Tobitt, 2020).

As in the United Kingdom, a study on news media diversity garnered coverage and debate in Australia, where both journalists and news sources were found to be predominantly white and male. As with the British analysis, the *Who Gets to Tell Australian Stories* report was conducted at the height of BLM awareness and coverage but examined broadcast content only. The research showed that only six per cent of presenters and sources were either "Indigenous or non-European," and at Channel Nine, only three per cent of on-air talent was from a non-European background (SBS News, 2020). One commentator chided the lack of diversity by asserting "cows were better represented…than people of colour." Channel Nine also received complaints over the comments of a conservative politician who – in an interview with an Indigenous host – described residents of a Melbourne public housing complex as "'drug addicts' and 'alcoholics' before claiming they were unable to speak English," driving the station to drop the politician as a regular commentator on the show (Eden, 2020). ABC's top political program, *Insiders*, was blasted for an all-white panel discussion on the BLM movement. In fact, it was later learned, the program had *never* featured a commentator of Indigenous or non-European background (Zhou, 2020).

Melbourne newspaper *The Age* was also chastised for its coverage of BLM protests, and journalists at the newspaper spoke out about politicization and pressure to take certain angles on their stories. An editorial claiming "Australia does not have a legacy of slavery" garnered a correction nine days later, but another story suggesting activists were "planning trouble" for police at an upcoming protest – without anything to corroborate the allegation – prompted news staff to act (Meade, 2020). Almost 70 journalists wrote a letter to the newspaper's executives raising concerns and decrying the organization's lack of diversity, noting that there had only been one Indigenous reporter in *The Age*'s 166-year history. Editor Alex Lavelle resigned a few days later. By contrast, when a Sky News host and News Corp. columnist wrote a column in the *Sunday Telegraph* in which he included the sentence "The reality in this country – and the US – is that the greatest danger to aborigines and negroes is themselves," he faced no consequences, despite a petition calling for him to be fired (Williams, 2020).

Conclusion

The death of George Floyd spawned much more than global protests. It raised the issue of systemic racism, initially with respect to law enforcement but then more broadly, forcing a racial reckoning in all institutions and across borders and oceans. In the case of news media, it is clear from this chapter that few organizations escaped scrutiny, much of it forced by journalists, particularly journalists of color, racialized or Indigenous, who endure discrimination inside and outside their newsrooms on a continual basis. Despite decades of organizational promises to boost diversity and educate white workers and supervisors on colonial history and systemic racism, progress had been woefully halting. However, with the momentum of the racial reckoning, racialized and Indigenous journalists called out their industry and employers for the obfuscation of the past, noting the damage it had done. Through their agency, they spelled out with force and clarity the issues that they have been facing. The next chapter chronicles their views, experiences, and frustrations based on the interviews, op-eds, personal essays, and first-person accounts they shared on a range of digital media platforms through much of 2020, and considers what their assertions mean for journalism in the 21st century.

References

Ali, Y. (2020, June 13). *'To Say That She's An Abusive Figure Is An Understatement': At ABC News, Toxicity Thrives.* Retrieved December 10, 2020, from Huffington Post: https://www.huffingtonpost.ca/entry/abc-news-toxicity-thrives_n_5ee3db80c5b684a0c4f2e297?ri18n=true

Balkissoon, D. (2020, June 17). *I tried to talk to my bosses about racism at work.* Retrieved July 5, 2020, from Chatelaine: https://www.chatelaine.com/opinion/racism-at-work/.

Bennett, D. (2020, September 19). *The reality and the hope.* Retrieved October 8, 2020, from Sportsnet: https://www.sportsnet.ca/more/facing-sports-medias-damaging-lack-diversity/.

Black Lives Matter. (2021, February 18). *About.* Retrieved from Black Lives Matter: https://blacklivesmatter.com/about/.

Buchanan, L., Bui, Q., & Patel, J. K. (2020, July 3). *Black Lives Matter may be the largest movement in U.S. history.* Retrieved from The New York Times: https://www.nytimes.com/interactive/2020/07/03/us/george-floyd-protests-crowd-size.html.

Canadaland. (2020, June 2). *Our stand in solidarity.* Retrieved from Twitter: https://twitter.com/CANADALAND/status/1267922662724186112.

CBC News. (2020a, June 26). *Black CBC journalist present when Wendy Mesley used N-word says her presence prompted disciplinary action.* Retrieved from cbc. ca: https://www.cbc.ca/news/canada/wendy-mesley-weekly-imani-walker-1.5629414.

CBC News. (2020b, September 18). *Mi'kmaw journalist assesses media coverage of fisheries dispute.* Retrieved from CBC News: https://www.cbc.ca/news/canada/nova-scotia/media-coverage-indigenous-issues-mi-kmaw-fishery-marshall-decision-1.5730472.

Chan, S. (2020, October 8). *To move forward on racial equity, newsrooms need to reckon with their pasts.* Retrieved from Nieman Reports: https://niemanreports.org/articles/to-move-forward-on-racial-equity-newsrooms-need-to-reckon-with-their-pasts/.

Chavez, N. (2020, December 16). *2020: The year America confronted racism.* Retrieved from CNN: https://www.cnn.com/interactive/2020/12/us/america-racism-2020/.

Cheung, A. (2020a, June 11). Retrieved July 13, 2020, from twitter.com: https://twitter.com/adrianwkcheung/status/1271196783943843840.

Cheung, H. (2020b, June 8). *George Floyd death: Why US protests are so powerful this time.* Retrieved from BBC News: https://www.bbc.com/news/world-us-canada-52969905.

Cotton, T. (2020, June 3). *Tom Cotton: Send in the troops.* Retrieved from The New York Times: https://www.nytimes.com/2020/06/03/opinion/tom-cotton-protests-military.html.

Craig, T. (2020, September 3). *'The United States is in crisis': Report tracks thousands of summer protests, most nonviolent.* Retrieved from The Washington Post: https://www.washingtonpost.com/national/the-united-states-is-in-crisis-report-tracks-thousands-of-summer-protests-most-nonviolent/2020/09/03/b43c359a-edec-11ea-99a1-71343d03bc29_story.html.

Cunneen, C. (2020, September 30). *"The torment of our powerlessness": Police violence against aboriginal people in Australia.* Retrieved from Harvard International Review: https://hir.harvard.edu/police-violence-australia-aboriginals/.

Devlin, K., Silver, L., Huang, C., Kent, N., & Connaughton, A. (2020, August 4). *Outside U.S., Floyd's killing and protests sparked discussion on legislators' Twitter accounts.* Retrieved from Pew Research Center: https://www.pewresearch.org/fact-tank/2020/08/04/outside-u-s-floyds-killing-and-protests-sparked-discussion-on-legislators-twitter-accounts/.

Eden, G. (2020, August 17). *Karl Stefanovic under fire after comments on media diversity report.* Retrieved from SBS News: https://www.sbs.com.au/news/the-feed/karl-stefanovic-under-fire-after-comments-on-media-diversity-report.

Edwards, F., Hedwig, L., & Esposito, M. (2019, August 20). *Risk of being killed by police use of force in the United States by age, race–ethnicity, and sex.* Retrieved from Proceedings of the National Academy of Sciences of the United States of America: https://www.pnas.org/content/116/34/16793.

Ellis, N. T. (2020, December 22). *Popular culture made it impossible to ignore America's reckoning with racism in 2020.* Retrieved from CNN: https://www.cnn.com/2020/12/18/us/systemic-racism-pop-culture-2020/index.html.

Farhi, P., & Ellison, S. (2020, June 13). *Ignited by public protests, American newsrooms are having their own racial reckoning.* Retrieved from The Washington Post: https://www.washingtonpost.com/lifestyle/media/ignited-by-public-protests-american-newsrooms-are-having-their-own-racial-reckoning/2020/06/12/be622bce-a995-11ea-94d2-d7bc43b26bf9_story.html.

Folkenflik, D. (2020, June 15). *Rancor erupts in 'LA Times' newsroom over race, equity and protest coverage.* Retrieved July 1, 2020, from NPR: https://www.npr.org/2020/06/15/874530954/rancor-erupts-in-la-times-newsroom-over-race-equity-and-protest-coverage.

Goldsbie, J. (2020a, June 9). *Wendy Mesley suspended from hosting duties after using "word that should never be used".* Retrieved from Canadaland: https://www.canadaland.com/wendy-mesley-suspended-from-the-weekly/.

Goldsbie, J. (2020b, August 26). *"Degrading and aggressive": Star newsroom rises up against Rosie DiManno.* Retrieved from Canadaland: https://www.canadaland.com/toronto-star-newsroom-rises-up-against-rosie-dimanno/.

Gramlich, J. (2019, April 30). *The gap between the number of blacks and whites in prison is shrinking.* Retrieved from Pew Research Center: https://www.pewresearch.org/fact-tank/2019/04/30/shrinking-gap-between-number-of-blacks-and-whites-in-prison/.

Hudson, S. (2020, June 18). *Canadian media has failed Black people.* Retrieved from Passage: https://readpassage.com/canadian-media-has-failed-black-people/.

Humphries, S. (2020, June 18). *Racial protests prompt waves of upheaval in America's newsrooms.* Retrieved from Christian Science Monitor: https://www.csmonitor.com/USA/Politics/2020/0618/Racial-protests-prompt-waves-of-upheaval-in-America-s-newsrooms.

John Howard Society. (2017, October 19). *Race, crime and justice in Canada.* Retrieved from John Howard Society: https://johnhoward.ca/blog/race-crime-justice-canada/.

Johnson, A. (2020, May 31). *@alexisjreports.* Retrieved from Twitter: https://twitter.com/alexisjreports/status/1267081467731103749?ref_src=twsrc%5Etfw%7Ctwcamp%5Etweetembed%7Ctwterm%5E1267081467731103749%7Ctwgr%5E%7Ctwcon%5Es1_&ref_url=https%3A%2F%2Fwww.pghcitypaper.com%2Fpittsburgh%2Fpittsburgh-post-gazette-removes-a-blac.

Koram, K. (2020, June 4). *Systemic racism and police brutality are British problems too.* Retrieved from The Guardian: https://www.theguardian.com/commentisfree/2020/jun/04/systemic-racism-police-brutality-british-problems-black-lives-matter.

Krishnan, M. (2020, August 20). *In the midst of a race reckoning, global news laid off some of its most vocal internal critics.* Retrieved September 2, 2020, from vice.com: https://www.vice.com/en/article/jgx4ek/in-the-midst-of-a-race-reckoning-global-news-laid-off-some-of-its-most-vocal-internal-critics.

Leazenby, L., & Polk, M. (2020, September 3). *What you need to know about Black Lives Matter in 10 questions.* Retrieved from Chicago Tribune: https://www.chicagotribune.com/lifestyles/ct-life-cb-black-lives-matter-chicago-20200903-xh75kbw5nfdk5joudlsgb2viwq-story.html.

Lowery, W. (2020, June 23). *A reckoning over objectivity, led by black journalists.* Retrieved July 7, 2020, from New York Times: https://www.nytimes.com/2020/06/23/opinion/objectivity-black-journalists-coronavirus.html.

McBain, S. (2020, June 12). *A moment of reckoning for the US media.* Retrieved September 9, 2020, from New Statesman: https://www.newstatesman.com/world/2020/06/black-lives-matter-us-media-new-york-times-bias-impartial.

McGregor, J. (2020, July 15). *Diversity job openings fell nearly 60% after the coronavirus. Then came the Black Lives Matter protests.* Retrieved December 8, 2020, from The Washington Post: https://www.washingtonpost.com/business/2020/07/15/diversity-jobs-coronavirus-george-floyd-protests/.

Meade, A. (2020, June 14). *Journalists at the Age express alarm over increasing politicisation and loss of independence.* Retrieved from The Guardian: https://www.theguardian.com/media/2020/jun/14/journalists-at-the-age-express-alarm-over-increasing-politicisation-and-loss-of-independence.

Murphy, J. (2020, July 30). *Billions have been raised for racial equity groups - what comes next?* Retrieved from BBC News: https://www.bbc.com/news/world-us-canada-53284611.

NBA.com. (2020, September 17). *End of season: Masai Ujiri - September 17, 2020.* Retrieved from NBA.com: https://www.nba.com/raptors/video/teams/raptors/2020/09/17/3424535/1600374768620-nba-prs-200917-masaieos-3424535.

Newman-Bremang, K. (2020, July 7). *For black women in media, a "dream job" is a myth.* Retrieved August 14, 2020, from Refinery 29: https://www.refinery29.com/en-ca/2020/07/9878117/systemic-racism-canadian-media.

O'Toole, E. (2020, June 12). *BBC bosses tell journalists they can't back Black Lives Matter campaign.* Retrieved from The National: https://www.thenational.scot/news/18515170.bbc-bosses-tell-journalists-cant-back-black-lives-matter-campaign/.

Romine, T. (2020, June 7). *Pittsburgh newspaper accused of removing black journalist from protest coverage after she posted a tweet about looting.* Retrieved December 10, 2020, from CNN: https://www.cnn.com/2020/06/07/us/pittsburgh-newspaper-black-journalist-looting-tweet/index.html.

SBS News. (2020, August 17). *The lack of cultural diversity in Australian TV news has been revealed in a new report.* Retrieved from SBS News: https://www.sbs.com.au/news/the-lack-of-cultural-diversity-in-australian-tv-news-has-been-revealed-in-a-new-report.

Smith, B. (2020, June 7). *THE media equation: inside the revolts erupting in America's big newsrooms.* Retrieved July 13, 2020, from New York Times: https://www.nytimes.com/2020/06/07/business/media/new-york-times-washington-post-protests.html.

Staples, B. (2020, June 4). Retrieved August 8, 2020, from Twitter: https://twitter.com/BrentNYT/status/1268541141416325121.

Stelkia, K. (2020, July 15). *Police brutality in Canada: A symptom of structural racism and colonial violence.* Retrieved from Yellowhead Institute: https://yellowheadinstitute.org/2020/07/15/police-brutality-in-canada-a-symptom-of-structural-racism-and-colonial-violence/#1594737656324-06d5bcedddde.

Subramaniam, V. (2020, June 2). *Vanmala Subramaniam: before you declare Canada is not a racist country, do your homework.* Retrieved July 13, 2020, from National Post: https://nationalpost.com/opinion/vanmala-subramaniam-before-you-declare-canada-is-not-a-racist-country-do-your-homework.

Szklarski, C. (2020, July 8). *Calls grow for news outlets reporting on systemic racism to address own failures.* Retrieved from CTV News: https://www.ctvnews.ca/canada/calls-grow-for-news-outlets-reporting-on-systemic-racism-to-address-own-failures-1.5016691.

The Guardian. (2020, May 29). *Black CNN reporter arrested on air at protests over George Floyd killing.* Retrieved from The Guardian: https://www.theguardian.com/us-news/2020/may/29/black-cnn-reporter-arrested-on-air-minneapolis-protests-george-floyd-killing.

Tobitt, C. (2020, June 24). *Fifty ethnic minority journalists urge faster action on diversity in newsrooms.* Retrieved from Press Gazette: https://www.pressgazette.co.uk/fifty-ethnic-minority-journalists-urge-faster-action-on-diversity-in-newsrooms/.

Wagner, L., & Strachan, M. (2020, July 1). *What went wrong at the Los Angeles Times.* Retrieved from Vice News: https://www.vice.com/en/article/v7g34y/what-went-wrong-at-the-los-angeles-times.

WashPostPR. (2020, June 18). *The Washington Post announces more than a dozen newsroom positions to be focused on race, including Managing Editor for Diversity and Inclusion.* Retrieved from The Washington Post: https://www.washingtonpost.com/pr/2020/06/18/washington-post-announces-more-than-dozen-newsroom-positions-be-focused-race-including-managing-editor-diversity-inclusion/.

Waterson, J. (2020, September 17). *BBC Newsnight accused over failure to interview any BAME guests for a week.* Retrieved from The Guardian: https://www.theguardian.com/world/2020/sep/17/shocking-lack-of-racial-diversity-and-women-in-uk-journalism-report.

White, N. (2020a, August 28). *Exclusive: BBC staff accuse corporation of being 'institutionally racist'.* Retrieved from Huffington Post UK: https://www.huffingtonpost.co.uk/amp/entry/bbc-institutionally-racist_uk_5f3f9c78c5b697824f977779/?__twitter_impression=true&guccounter=-2&guce_referrer=aHR0cHM6Ly93d3cudGhlZ3VhcmRpYW4uY29tL2N2bWVlbnpc2ZyZWUvMjAyMC9zZXNAVMDIvYmxhY2stam91cm5hbGlzdC1layltZWR-GlzdC11ayltZWWR.

White, N. (2020b, August 29). *Exclusive: black BBC staff morale at 'All time low' after N-word scandal.* Retrieved from Huffington Post UK: https://www.huffingtonpost.co.uk/entry/bbc-n-word-staff-morale-low_uk_5f43f0a8c5b66a80ee1621f6.

Williams, C. (2020, June 15). *Peter Gleeson stuns by using 'racist' language in Black Lives Matter opinion piece.* Retrieved from Huffington Post Australia: https://www.huffingtonpost.com.au/entry/peter-gleeson-petition-to-be-sacked-opinion-piece_au_5ee6e186c5b64e087259e477.

Women in Journalism. (2020, September 16). *A week in British newsrooms.* Retrieved from Women in Journalism: https://womeninjournalism.co.uk/lack-diversity-british-newsrooms/.

Zhou, N. (2020, June 28). *'It dampens the conversation': no more excuses for Australian media's lack of diversity.* Retrieved from The Guardian: https://www.theguardian.com/media/2020/jun/28/it-dampens-the-conversation-no-more-excuses-for-australian-medias-lack-of-diversity.

2 In Their Own Words

Journalism and the "White Normative View" of the World

Introduction

In the scholarship of race and news media, researchers are invariably obliged to at least make passing reference to a report by the National Advisory Commission on Civil Disorders in the United States, led by Illinois Governor Otto Kerner Jr. in 1968. The panel of nine white and two Black men was assembled to determine the causes of rebellion in Black urban areas at the time (Byerly & Wilson, 2009). The group came to be known as the Kerner Commission, and its blunt conclusions, shocked white America: "...white society is deeply implicated in the ghetto. White institutions created it, white institutions maintain it, and white society condones it" (National Advisory Commission on Civil Disorders, 1968, cited in Kendi, 2016, p. 404). The failings of mainstream news media were a central theme, and the report expressly called for the hiring of Black reporters and editors, noting that "the press has too long basked in a white world looking out at it, if at all, with white men's eyes, and white perspective" (p. 404).

More than 50 years later, after decades of hiring, mentorship, and diversity initiatives, that same conclusion seems as relevant as ever, and not just in the United States. In the racial reckoning described in Chapter 1, non-white journalists raised their voices as never before, directing their criticism at a fourth estate that has failed to fully embrace the Kerner Commission's calls for more than the "white perspective." In an unprecedented and often blunt assessment of their industry's response to global Black Lives Matter (BLM) protests of police brutality, journalists who identify as Black, Indigenous, or as people of color, shared examples of the hypocrisy, double standards, and racial ignorance of their employers and industry. They did this in social media posts, first-person opinion pieces, blog entries, media interviews, and in a variety of digital media forums, despite the risk such candor

DOI: 10.4324/9781003261544-3

could bring to their careers. In so doing they have documented the failure of journalism's ethical canon to speak truth to issues of race; they detailed the inadequacy of diversity and inclusion initiatives; they laid bare the culture of white supremacy, racism, and microaggression in newsrooms; they underscored the burden of representation placed on racialized staff, whereby they are expected to lead diversity initiatives and serve as "sensitivity readers" on stories related to race, but considered biased when it comes to covering those same issues; and they shared their hopes and visions for a better approach to journalism.

This chapter captures and examines those insights offered by Indigenous and racialized journalists, primarily in the United States and Canada, but also in Australia and the United Kingdom through the period following the death of George Floyd in 2020. A content analysis breaks down the data into two overarching categories. The first is systemic racism and news content, reflected in themes that include objectivity's contradictory role as a white, normative lens; an abiding ignorance of racism; and news coverage that tends to minimize discrimination, sensationalize, and stereotype racialized and Indigenous Peoples. The second category, systemic racism and the work environment, emerges through themes of the burden on non-white staff to lead diversity initiatives; accusations of bias and activism; the lack of diversity among staff, supervisors, and managers; microaggressions; and the stress, exhaustion, and mental health issues experienced by racialized staff. A quick description of the study's methodology is followed by an exploration of those categories and themes, relying on the words of the Black, racialized, and Indigenous journalists who shared their perspectives through the sample period. The content analysis did not include data from the United Kingdom and Australia; however, an overview of the media accounts of Black, Indigenous, Asian, and minority ethnic journalists from both countries are discussed in a separate section. The views of all these journalists are then interpreted through the theoretical lenses of post-colonialism and critical race theory, exposing the systemic racism on which journalism evolved. The findings affirm the assertion that Journalism's ethical canon and norms of practice are based on white dominance. However, in contrast to the Kerner recommendations 50 years earlier, the words of racialized and Indigenous journalists articulate pathways to reform, beyond simplistic hiring initiatives.

Analyzing the Racial Reckoning

As the BLM movement grew and gained momentum, and as demands for racial justice were leveled at all institutions, it became clear that journalism too, was going to be held to account by its own racialized and Indigenous workers, and their allies. What they said, and what it meant for the way journalism has traditionally been practiced, was clearly a rich vein of inquiry, and so this study was launched. Data collection began by regularly searching the internet and news databases in the United States and Canada for content produced by racialized news staff related to journalism and race, a purposive sampling approach. However, as most of these media accounts referenced work by other authors or issues at other organizations, with links to additional articles, documents, or social media, snowball sampling added to the data set. The content units for the analysis were defined as first-person reflections of the interplay between race and news media and had to meet the criterion of being created by journalistic authors who identify as Black, Indigenous, as a person of color, or as otherwise racialized. In a handful of cases, articles or transcripts of interviews were included in which the sources/interviewees met the ethnic background requirements and were speaking to issues of race and journalism. Additionally, some Twitter threads were included as sources of authentic discussion by Indigenous and racialized journalists. However, most content units were textual articles published by mainstream media, journalism-focused organizations such as the Nieman Lab and the Poynter Institute, or the websites of organizations associated with racial justice. The sample period extends from May to the end of December 2020. In total 84 content units (comprising 145,000 words) were captured including 69 textual articles, nine Twitter threads, and six digital media interviews (podcasts or YouTube). The content analysis began with an initial consideration of all the content units. Inductive category development was used to identify keywords and establish codes to guide the analysis. Codes were compared to establish relationships and create clusters, and then reorganized to determine categories and themes. At the same time, examples were identified in the data to illustrate the concept connected to each category and theme.

As an additional research tool, text-mining software WordStat8 was deployed to address some of the subjectivity associated with the sampling methods and inductive categorization. Text-mining allows for the compilation of "concepts based on the lexicon of the text but which can be weighted according to word frequency and which take account of elementary word associations" (Prior, 2014, p. 367). The software identified keywords, and determined topics and phrases based on word associations. While this does assist to "get a grip on the strength of the relationships between the concepts" in the text, it does not explain "what the various narratives contained within the documents might be" (Prior, 2014, p. 368). That deeper analysis of the content units is explored at length in the findings below, but text-mining did corroborate the categories and themes determined in the initial analysis.

Undoubtedly this is a somewhat unconventional research design. However, as with content analysis generally, this work is based on an unobtrusive selection of data where "the researcher does not 'intrude' on what is being studied and thus does not affect the outcome of the research" (Berger, 2000, p. 181). The data set is comprised entirely of the voices of racialized and Indigenous journalists at a critical moment in time, and offers detailed description and insight. As Stewart (2016) points out: "The goal of a qualitative study is believability, based on coherence, insight, and instrumental utility (Eisner, 1991) and trust-worthiness (Lincoln & Guba, 1985), achieved through a process of verification rather than through conventionally privileged quantitative validity measures" (p. 260).

The two overarching categories related to journalism that emerged are: race and news practice, and systemic racism in the journalistic workplace. The first category is further broken down into these themes: objectivity's contradictory role as a white, normative view on the world; ignorance of racial history and experiences; stereotypic coverage; and a tendency to minimize or downplay racism. The second category, systemic racism and the work environment, consists of these themes: the burden of leading diversity initiatives; accusations of bias and activism; the lack of diversity among staff, supervisors, and managers; constant microaggressions; and the stress, exhaustion, and mental health issues experienced by racialized staff. The text-mining software corroborated the significance of these themes in the prevalence of the keywords, phrases, and topics it identified.

Race and News Practice: "White Normative" Ethics

Time and again, Indigenous and racialized journalists over the sample period cited notions of objectivity as a constant source of friction between newsroom managers and racialized reporters. Some referenced it as neutrality, (false) balance, impartiality, bias, or "both-sides-ism" but the overwhelming conclusion of these reporters is that journalism's central ethic is universally applied through the lens of whiteness. Former *Washington Post* journalist and Pulitzer Prize winner Wesley Lowery, writing in *The New York Times*, explained that whiteness is "accepted as the objective neutral. When Black and brown reporters and editors challenge those conventions, it is not uncommon for them to be pushed out, reprimanded or robbed of new opportunities" (Lowery, 2020). He also weighed in on the *Times'* Tom Cotton op-ed controversy, specifically challenging ethical orthodoxy, posting on Twitter that the "American view-from-nowhere, 'objectivity'-obsessed, both-sides journalism is a failed experiment... We need to rebuild our industry as one that operates from a place of moral clarity" (Smith, 2020). A *Times* journalist of color, Brent Staples, also referenced objectivity as "the white normative view" of the world, noting that early in his career he had been accused of "pushing a Black agenda" (Staples, 2020). In Canada, Denise Balkissoon, faced similar scrutiny at the national newspaper where she worked, when the head of the editorial board told her that her "ideology" precluded her from being a board member herself (Balkissoon, 2020). A Canadian television producer and journalist, Sadiya Ansari, described her experiences working on a daytime talk show, where at story meetings she and other women of color were scolded that "'it's not about race,' that we lack objectivity, that a story simply doesn't have an audience," or more specifically, a *white* audience (Ansari, 2020).

The contradictory application of ethics between racialized and white staffers was cited often. Waubgeshig Rice, an Anishnaabe writer and journalist from Wasauksing First Nation in Ontario, wrote "They'll call your objectivity into question and doubt your capability to cover Indigenous-related stories just because of who you are. Paradoxically, they may not let you cover anything else" (Rice, 2020). The pressure to bring a white perspective to story selection and other editorial decisions is pervasive in the data. As he was writing his own piece on race and news media in *Nieman Reports*, Isaac Bailey confessed he became concerned about sounding "alarmist," but needed to share the "cold, hard, uncomfortable truth" that everyone – including him – is influenced "by white supremacy," and though "it might be difficult for many journalists to accept, it is not a slur to speak that truth aloud" (Bailey, 2020).

Coverage of BLM demonstrations provided Indigenous and racialized journalists with ample opportunity to consider the industry's body of work, and police and crime reporting more broadly. The prevailing view in the data is that white normative objectivity enables one-sided and superficial coverage. Criticism often focused on sources and word choice. At *The Philadelphia Inquirer*, publisher of the infamous "Buildings Matter, Too" headline, Solomon Jones noted the publication's reporting on addiction over the years, whereby its position on safe injection sites shifted from opposition to support as "statistics showed that those suffering drug overdoses were mostly white" (Jones, 2020).

He advocated an approach to news that treats "African Americans as human beings with stories to be told rather than characters with drama to be exploited" (Jones, 2020). Photojournalism practices that support the white, dominant narrative were also cited for their lack of context, and the erasure of the lived experience of racialized groups. When images are chosen with a focus on "destruction and conflict," photojournalists and editors "leave behind countless other images that signify what this moment is about for the people who live with oppression every day" (Elian, 2020). Visual journalist David "Dee" Delgado describes contrasting approaches with a white photographer at a BLM event in Brooklyn, and how they each treated a drunk and agitated Black protester.

> The white photographer is looking at him like an instigator, a troublemaker, and I'm not looking at him that way," Delgado says. "I'm looking at him as, this is a guy that's hurt, and he has no other way to vocalize that hurt but with rage. [The white photojournalists] started photographing him angry and trying to antagonize the crowd. I photographed him when the crowd was calming him down and talking to him and telling him that that wasn't the way. [White photojournalists are] only looking for the anarchy."
>
> Elian (2020)

Pacinthe Mattar, recounted an incident from before the reckoning while working for the CBC, when she was covering protests in Baltimore over the police killing of Freddie Gray in 2015. She interviewed two young Black men who shared their personal stories of police abuse, but was stunned to find her executive producer more concerned about the police department's position on the allegations, and insisted on absolute verification of her two sources, questioning whether they had given Mattar their real names: "That's when I learned that, in Canadian media, there's an added burden of proof, for both journalists and sources, that accompanies stories about racism" (Mattar, 2020). When the final report of the national inquiry into Missing and Murdered Indigenous Women and Girls in Canada was released, an Indigenous journalist was told by a white editor to remove the word "genocide" from her story, even though it was a direct quote from the actual document. In fact, mainstream media spent more time focused on the word "genocide" in the report than on the contents, "derailing" the critical work of the inquiry, and "taking the urgency and accountability out of the conversation" (Fowler & Pulfer, 2020).

The double standard wrought by notions of white normative objectivity identified in the data is reflected in examples where (white) editors advocate for cautious word choice around state-run institutions and policies but graphic representations of marginalized groups living on reserves (reservations in the United States) or in the inner city; the word "genocide" is edited out of copy, but gritty, if superficial and sensational depictions of addiction are encouraged. Erika Dilday, used the term "POCporn" to describe the narrative, which she says is "like poverty porn and other types of superficial coverage" in that "it focuses on the shock value of situations and the 'otherness' of marginalized communities, allowing armchair middle-class audiences to reinforce the stereotypes they already have of 'those people' and 'those places'" (Dilday, 2020). Hadeel Abdel-Nabi echoed that sentiment, pointing out that "the experiences of marginalized communities are whittled down to either trauma or fables of 'defying the odds.' Sources become wells of potential stories or quotes from which white reporters can over-extract, rather than human beings" (Abdel-Nabi, 2020).

There were also examples where a white lens on the world reflected an abject ignorance of racial experiences, or missed important historical background on a marginalized group that rendered media narratives untrue. *The New York Times* columnist Paul Krugman suggested on Twitter that the September 11th attacks did not lead to "a mass outbreak of anti-Muslim sentiment and violence" prompting responses on social media and news sites pointing out that Islamophobic hate crimes spiked after 9-11 (Haltiwanger, 2020). Coverage of First Nation fishing rights on Canada's Atlantic coast brought criticism of mainstream news coverage for its failure to provide the historical context of treaty law. Non-Indigenous fishermen harassed Mi'kmaw lobster crews on the water and on land, and even set fire to a lobster pound containing the Mi'kmaw catch. The Mi'kmaq were engaged in a "moderate livelihood" lobster fishery outside the non-Indigenous season as guaranteed by centuries-old treaties and legal precedent established by the Supreme Court of Canada. Non-Indigenous fishermen claimed the Mi'kmaw harvest would ruin the lobster stock. However, reporting on the issue suggested the Mi'kmaw actions were illegal, that their rights were in dispute. A Mi'kmaw video journalist with APTN, Trina Roache, set the record straight on the Canadaland podcast, observing that the media need to understand that the Mi'kmaq are not an interest group, "they are the First Peoples, they are a sovereign nation with jurisdiction and if you don't get that, then you end up with that he-said, she-said minimizing the Mi'kmaw authority in the situation" (Roache, 2020).

Several writers singled out headlines that reflected a white-normative, positive bias toward police, and a negative bias toward protesters. Kendra Pierre-Louis referenced "A night of fire and fury across America as protests intensify" from *The Washington Post,* and *The New York Times*' "Appeals for calm as sprawling protests threaten to spiral out of control," asserting they "focus exclusively on the violence of the protests. They don't tell us where the violence is coming from," (Pierre-Louis, 2020). Writing in *The Atlantic,* Sarah Jackson cited *BuzzFeed*'s "bizarre wordsmithery" with this headline, "15 Not-Peaceful Things the Cops Were Recorded Doing During This Weekend's Black Lives Matter Protests," noting that "not-peaceful" was a "euphemism for violent"; but she also observed a shift in some mainstream news organizations who stepped away from "representations of blame" as well as the "assumptions that result from an unbalanced reliance on police as sources" (Jackson, 2020). She offered examples from NBC News, "U.S. Police Failing to Respect Right to Peaceful Protest," and her own publication's "When Police View Citizens as Enemies" as evidence that headlines can be forthright and accurate. Other writers in the sample noted the way passive language was used to describe police actions, deflecting responsibility for violence against protesters.

While a few journalists offered examples of excellent news content, no one advocated for the status quo in discussing the application of ethics or established reporting norms. In sum, the prevailing view in the data is that newsgathering as it is currently practiced does as much to maintain racism, as it does to expose it.

Systemic Racism and the Work Environment

Under this category, the data reveal much about what it is like to work in newsrooms for racialized and Indigenous workers. The journalists behind the data made frequent reference to the general lack of diversity in news staff and management, and its impact on editorial decisions, news content, and staff relations. They spoke to the racism they experienced, the microaggressions, the lack of advancement, and the pay inequity. They described poorly resourced, ineffective diversity measures, which came with the expectation that they would lead such efforts. And they detailed the stress and mental health issues related to the difficult work of covering racism in their own communities.

In the previous section the impact of predominantly white leadership and staff in newsrooms was evident in a variety of editorial contexts, resulting in an approach to newsgathering devoid of racial context and history. That lack of inclusive leadership represents an ongoing challenge summed up succinctly in a Twitter thread by investigative journalist Martha Troian, from Obishikokaang (Lac Seul First Nation) in northwestern Ontario, describing her experiences in which she has had to "explain & re-explain the importance of an Indigenous story or issue to a non-Indigenous journalist/editor, or to a group. Honestly, it's tiring" (Troian, 2020). She finds well-intentioned non-Indigenous editors bring "their white eye lens" with the effect of hampering "the vetting process or your story will become sanitized."

As a result of such encounters, the need for much stronger representation of Indigenous and racialized journalists and senior editors in news organizations was one of the strongest messages to emerge from the data. The views of individual news staff were laid out by CBC morning show host Christine Genier (2020), a Ta'an Kwäch'än citizen, who, as noted in Chapter 1, resigned in frustration over the suppression of Indigenous and Black voices at the public broadcaster in June. She urged the CBC to hire more racialized and Indigenous producers, hosts, and reporters (Hong, 2020). Throughout the data there are references to past diversity initiatives that have failed to deliver substantive results. Greg Braxton, writing in the *Los Angeles Times*, states that the "cultural climate of the newspaper is still troubling" and as "the most senior African American journalist" at the newspaper "there are so few who look like me, and there is almost no one who can relate to my present and past experience" (Braxton, 2020). There were references in the data to management acknowledging concerns about the lack of diversity by bringing in racialized staff on a contract or freelance basis, and the ensuing issues with job security and retention. The consistent message was to recruit more journalists of color, but at the same time, advised that there needs to be *more* than just hiring. Gabrielle Hickmon warned that "commitments to 'be better' without tangible plans of how to get to 'better' do more harm than good: they leave unaddressed what our experience is like once we are in the door" (Hickmon, 2020).

Those experiences are reflected in the data set as microaggressions, difficulty in advancing, inequitable remuneration, and being perceived as troublemakers. Writing on the Poynter Institute's website, Doris Truong listed some of the workplace issues: "The colleague who won't learn to pronounce our six-letter name but who can rattle off Shostakovich without pause. The stranger who touches our hair. The co-opting of our culture. The disrespect of our sacred icons" (Truong, 2020). Kathleen Newman-Bremang recounted an experience while working for a cable music channel in which a white colleague commented on her fellow on-air talent, "'Sometimes, I think he's hot, but then I remember he's Black.' The dehumanization of Black bodies was as ubiquitous as Marianas Trench music videos" (Newman-Bremang, 2020).

While these journalists experience racism in their workplace, they are also often expected to lead efforts to address it, the data show. ESPN's Rob King wrote that "fostering racial equity in our newsrooms is our second full-time job," (King, 2020). The work of racial justice extends outside the newsroom, so that Sportsnet's Donnovan Bennett gets "five to 10 outside requests a day" for appearances and interviews (Bennett, 2020). "Being Black has become my beat, and I'm often covering it alone. As proud as I am of the work, I'd love some company, and I'd love to be considered an expert on something else for a change." The concern, often expressed, is that diversity work also has an impact on career advancement, so that "while we act as de facto diversity consultants, our white colleagues are busy with their actual jobs. Guess which work shows up as productivity that decision-makers value?" (Campbell, 2020).

The toll on mental health from living in racist society, coupled with covering the violence against racialized and Indigenous Peoples, was a familiar concern. Danielle Belton explained how the emotional distance principle associated with journalistic objectivity offers no escape from the harsh reality of discrimination, "Because often, to white people, this is just another news story. For us, this is our lives…and our deaths, displayed for public consumption, often without context or understanding" (Belton, 2020). One editor, after the first weeks of BLM protests across North America, met with one of her writers to discuss assignments, and was told "Please don't assign me those kinds of stories for a while. I'm calling in Black" (Ali, 2020a, 2020b). NBC's Tracie Potts wrote that "racism, discrimination and police brutality elevated by Floyd's death are deeply personal for journalists of color" and that "mental health experts acknowledge that these incidents are emotionally devastating for African Americans" (Potts, 2020). For these journalists there is the additional burden of "hate mail and trolling" that for them tends to come as a racist flourish as well (Balkissoon, 2020).

Despite the challenges documented through all these accounts, the journalists represented in the data consistently acknowledged their commitment to ensure momentum toward real change, a resilience in the face of systemic racism, a unified voice for media workers marginalized for too long. CBC anchor Adrian Harewood described the moment:

> The ground is shifting beneath our feet because we are speaking up and out, without fear, because we know we are telling the truth.

We need to keep up the pressure. Keep on raising our voices. Keep on challenging power in the spaces we occupy. Every bit of action and engagement counts.

Harewood (2020)

Journalists Respond to the Reckoning in the United Kingdom and Australia

Chapter 1 reviewed the debate and discussion sparked by BLM in British and Australian news media. The outpouring of published accounts by racialized and Indigenous journalists holding the industry to account was not as prolific as in North America, but the experiences, frustrations, and calls for reform were strikingly similar, and also break down into the overarching categories of racism's impact on content, and the workplace.

As with the North American data, the lack of diversity in British newsrooms was linked to the racial blind spots and ignorance of the history and lived experience of racialized peoples. Niellah Arboine, recognized the disproportionate impact of COVID-19 on Black people but noted that "only a handful of Black journalists were present at the daily briefings asking those important questions" (Arboine, 2020). As BLM demonstrations captured the imagination of the British public, Arboine asserted that the news media's discomfort with race was exposed: "Every week there was another reporting failure – famous Black people being mixed up, racist slurs voiced by white reporters, Black Lives Matter protests blamed for any future Covid-19 spikes."

In advocating for Black media, journalist and broadcaster Henry Bonsu described mainstream journalism's superficial treatment of race, and racialized news staff. "You often find yourself pulling your punches and not really saying the truth, because you know how it'll be presented," he said in an interview, adding that Black journalists are frequently treated "as a subject of tabloid debate rather than a participant in serious news reporting" (Batchelor-Hunt & Walawakar, 2020). Bonsu argued that when Black reporters are brought into serious discussions about colonialism or slavery it descends into "a bunfight, where the Black commentator is on trial."

JJ Anisiobi, deputy digital content director at *OK!* magazine online, is part of a new professional body formed through the reckoning, the Black British Media Society (BBMS). He became involved because the "lack of diversity in newsrooms leads to a one-sided narrative in all parts of the media scene. How can Black voices be heard and represented if there's no Black voice in the office space to be heard" (Melan Mag, 2020). He described the same double standard described by journalists in North America which manifests "all too often" in Britain as a "bias of some media to demonise Black celebrities and athletes yet praise white counterparts" who find themselves in the same circumstances. Nadine Batchelor-Hunt recognized the white normative bias in agenda-setting at the height of the BLM movement in the United Kingdom. On a day when activists across Britain were drawing attention to discrimination and its impact, the front pages of newspapers were filled with coverage of a new lead in the case of Madeleine McCann, the toddler who disappeared 13 years earlier when she and her parents were vacationing in Portugal. Batchelor-Hunt wrote that if "Black lives are going to matter – to truly matter – we must call out this pattern of behaviour in coverage like this," noting that while the McCann story was compelling, "The police brutality, inequality, and discrimination that Black people face in society should be making front page news, and if it isn't, we need to be interrogating the reasons why" (Batchelor-Hunt, 2020).

A workplace devoid of racial representation, and fraught with microaggression, disparate opportunities for advancement and mistrust emerged in accounts by Black and other racialized journalists, comparable to the data from the United States and Canada. Nadine White, whose Twitter page profile describes her as "UK's first & only Race Correspondent," reported extensively on the racial reckoning and the media, particularly on issues at the BBC. Racialized journalists, whose identities she protected, offered a frank view of their experiences in the newsroom. One source conceded that even for non-white staff in senior positions, "you're not trusted with your own judgement. You're 'helicopter checked' by white managers more often than not, who have final say over how stories are told" (White, 2020a, 2020b). Another source stated that "Management equate the colour of your skin to having low intelligence." A group of television workers, the Black, Asian and Minority Ethnic TV Task Force, captured the general sentiment of racialized media staff in an open letter to networks and streaming platforms detailing their workplace concerns and urging industry reforms. They described "the bleak reality of working in TV as a non-white person" covers a range of issues "from bullying to microaggressions and fears of being blacklisted," suggesting the industry is filled with "tokenism" and an "almost impenetrable glass ceiling at mid-level" (Melan Mag, 2020).

In Australia, news coverage and panel discussions of BLM triggered the same wave of criticism seen in North America and the United Kingdom. When ABC's *Insiders* gathered an all-white group of journalists to talk about the BLM movement, and it was subsequently revealed it had *never* featured a non-European or Indigenous panelist, host David Speers admitted the program "needs to do better" (Zhou, 2020). A week after the all-white panel *Insiders* featured ABC's European correspondent, Bridget Brennan, a Dja Dja Wurrung and Yorta Yorta woman, on the show. She spoke on-air about ABC's stark lack of diversity on the program, stating "it is not good enough anymore particularly at this moment, but I would say any week, to have a panel of white people speaking about issues when there is very little lived experience of discrimination and racism on that panel" (Insiders ABC, 2020). In another high-profile controversy, Channel Nine was forced to drop a regular feature with politician Pauline Hanson after she described public housing residents as addicts, alcoholics, and unable to speak English in an interview with Brooke Boney, a Gamilaroi woman (Gillespie, 2020). Boney explained why she found the comments so offensive:

> I grew up in housing commission. To me, I was thinking about all of those kids sitting at home watching, all of those people trapped in their apartments, watching and thinking, "This is what Australia thinks of us. This is what the rest of our country thinks – is that we're alcoholics and drug addicts."
>
> Gillespie (2020)

The coverage of BLM protests, particularly downplaying police violence and supporting the law enforcement narrative of protester violence, was singled out by news staff at *The Age*, as described in the previous chapter, and other news outlets. As seen in the North American data, oddly passive language in reference to police actions contrasted with descriptions of demonstrators as "savages." A notable BLM protest drawing attention to Indigenous deaths in custody was described as peaceful, resulted in only three arrests, but left a number of participants injured after police used pepper spray. One of the best examples of the passive voice was a Tweet and an on-screen chyron in a newscast, that stated "several protesters hit with capsicum [pepper] spray" (9News Australia, 2020). Of course, pepper spray has no agency, and as people noted on social media, the coverage avoids recognition of police complicity in protesters' injuries.

The string of media gaffes was documented by several Australian news organizations. Commenting on BLM, and the challenges of being Indigenous in a colonial nation, SBS journalist Nakari Thorpe explained, "White is seen as the norm. It is the standard voice. And that's not just in Australia, it goes beyond that. Whiteness is not even seen as a race sometimes" (Rudhran, 2020). Thorpe, a Gunnai, Gunditjmara and Gooreng Gooreng woman, described the same experiences felt by racialized journalists in other parts of the world, observing that the struggle for diversity in news organizations falls to people like her, "So often the onus is put on us, as Indigenous or non-white journalists, to change it, or to know what to do. It is exhausting. The change needs to come up from the top" (Zhou, 2020). She points out diversity is not the end in itself, but important for what it brings to journalism, namely truth and accuracy.

Journalism's Role in the Colonial, Exclusionary State

The systemic racism running through the application of journalistic ethics is the same force that makes the workplace such a challenge to navigate for journalists of color and Indigenous news staff. Allusions in the data to white dominance, white bias, the "white normative view," and white supremacy reflect the ongoing legacy of societies founded on colonialism and racial exclusion. The histories of racialized groups, people of color, and Indigenous Peoples and their experiences with discrimination are all distinct, but what they all have in common is the othering by Europeans, and the persistent expression of white superiority. White Europeans are uniformly cast as the "rational, virtuous, mature, 'normal'" standard of humanity (Said, 1978/2003, p. 40), against which all others are deemed inferior. In the mainstream news coverage of BLM protests, it is the demonstrators, often racialized, who are cast as irrational, violent, and abnormal. This phenomenon was captured in the data in some of the discussions related to headlines, and the use of the passive voice in reporting on police actions. Kendi maintains that historically, white negativity is individualized, while Black negativity is generalized, so that "negative behavior by any Black person became proof of what was wrong with Black people, while negative behavior by any white person only proved what was wrong with that person" (Kendi, 2016, pp. 42–43). In the news coverage of police brutality, both inside and outside the sample period of this study, this manifests in the "few bad apples" framing, when actual statistics support a systemic racism narrative.

The discussions of objectivity throughout the data perhaps best capture the anxiety, frustration, and anger of journalists in the sample with the uneven application of ethical standards. Former *Washington Post* journalist Wesley Lowery, cited earlier, was mentioned so often that his name comes up as a keyword in the text-mining. His frank appraisal of objectivity in today's journalism resonates with many racialized news staff, when he writes:

> Since American journalism's pivot many decades ago from an openly partisan press to a model of professed objectivity, the mainstream has allowed what it considers objective truth to be decided almost exclusively by white reporters and their mostly white bosses. And those selective truths have been calibrated to avoid offending the sensibilities of white readers. On opinion pages, the contours of acceptable public debate have largely been determined through the gaze of white editors.
>
> Lowery (2020)

The norms of practice in journalism developed alongside European colonial expansion, particularly in settler states, privileging voices of white authority in newsgathering, while under-representing the marginalized. When Indigenous and racialized reporters identify important stories in their communities, or challenge coverage that lacks historic or social context, the data show they are often met with accusations of bias. Objectivity is a white lens that serves to obscure the truth, and "functions as a blocking device, stopping the rigorous and informed examination of power in everyday journalistic practice," (Durham, 1998, cited in Callison & Young, 2020, p. 45). The "view from nowhere" is in fact, a view from white privilege, from white dominance, described in the data as "a tool of racial bias that establishes white norms as the measure of newsworthiness" (Douglas, 2020). Critical race theorists assert objectivity is a characteristic of white supremacy, reflected in a disdain for emotion and "impatience with any thinking that does not appear logical to those with power" (Jones & Okun, 2001).

The white normative lens can be subverted by decolonizing media practice, that is by taking the editorial decision-making out of the exclusive control of white gatekeepers, managers, editors, and reporters, and putting it in the hands of racialized and Indigenous journalists. A comparative analysis of mainstream television news with the Aboriginal Peoples Television Network (APTN) in Canada found that the Indigenous-run service was more diverse, more authentic, more balanced, and more accurate (Clark, 2014a, 2014b). In the United States, Black people have historically "found it necessary for their lived experiences to be authentically narrated through vehicles they control," giving rise to the Black press (Douglas, 2020). Black media, in contrast to the mainstream, provide news *for* the Black community, instead of *about*, "changing the lenses of victimization and dysfunction into lenses of empowerment and agency." With the power to control the means of news productions, Indigenous and racialized journalists can address the oft-cited concerns about superficial, sensational, and stereotypic coverage of their communities.

However, such power is inequitably distributed along racial lines in mainstream news organizations. Calls for comprehensive diversity initiatives that go beyond simple hiring were a common refrain in the data. The same systemic racism that has shaped news practice and content has not been addressed in work culture or human resources policies, including promotion, compensation, and mentoring. The people whose work makes up the data set often found irony in the apparent newsroom ethos of progressiveness and liberalism, even as white colleagues are ignorant and even dismissive of non-white cultures and experiences. Low participation rates for racialized and Indigenous news staff are not just a reflection of low hiring, but also of poor retention tied to inadequate supports and a failure to address microaggression. Francisco Vara-Orta, a former *San Antonio Express-News* journalist, now with Investigative Reporters and Editors, builds on that sense of irony in the recognition that journalism itself, as it exists today, contributes to the problem of racism in society. He states, "our job is to hold institutions to account, but we can't even do it within our own home – our newsrooms. That's absolutely demoralizing… it's horrible to look at the mirror and wonder where you've been complicit" (Miller, 2020).

Most news organizations have promised reform, though the steps taken so far fall on a wide continuum from resistance and defensiveness, to substantive changes. Moving forward, news managers need to understand systemic racism in a way they have not in the past; they need to understand that there are multiple audiences, not just white people; they need to accept and value difference; and they will have to welcome to the executive suite people who do not look like them, people of color, Black people, and Indigenous Peoples. More succinctly, they need to understand this maxim, from Kimberlé Crenshaw (1997): "treating different things the same can generate as much an inequality as treating the same things differently" (p. 285).

Conclusion

The racial reckoning in journalism has provided a rich and detailed model of the interplay between white privilege and dominance, race, and newsgathering norms. In sharing their experiences and insights Indigenous and racialized journalists have exposed the fallacy of journalism's coveted objectivity and directed the attention of news leaders to more authentic and equitable ethical ideals, truth and Wesley Lowery's "moral clarity." That means recognizing the historical context of discrimination and white bias, and privileging truth and accuracy over what so often turns out to be only the appearance of objectivity. The over-representation of white news staff continues to see the world "with white men's eyes," as the Kerner Commission asserted over five decades ago. The need for news media gatekeepers from racialized and Indigenous backgrounds remains acute. However, recruiting non-white news staff is only the first step, and the data point to a range of measures to ensure retention and workplace equity. In short, journalism has to change the way it is practiced, the ethical ideals that guide it, and the way it develops and supports journalists of color, and Black and Indigenous news staff. The analysis detailed in this chapter has identified the ways journalism struggles with race and provided examples of the resulting misrepresentation of Indigenous and racialized peoples at a particular moment in time, the racial reckoning of 2020. The next chapter builds on this analysis, seeking to explain why this is still the case, and where the opportunities for change might lie.

References

9News Australia. (2020, June 6). *#Breaking*. Retrieved from Twitter: https://twitter.com/9NewsAUS/status/1269199130427080704.

Abdel-Nabi, H. (2020, June 23). *The systemic racism of Canadian journalism*. Retrieved from The Sprawl: https://www.sprawlcalgary.com/bipoc-representation-in-local-newsrooms.

Ali, D. D. (2020a, September 15). *Newsrooms should make space for emotions*. Retrieved October 1, 2020, from Nieman Reports: https://niemanreports.org/articles/newsrooms-should-make-space-for-emotions/.

Ali, Y. (2020b, June 13). *'To say that she's an abusive figure is an understatement': at ABC news, toxicity thrives.* Retrieved December 10, 2020, from Huffington Post: https://www.huffingtonpost.ca/entry/abc-news-toxicity-thrives_n_5ee3db80c5b684a0c4f2e297?ri18n=true.

Ansari, S. (2020, July 3). *Canadian media is white AF — I want a mentor who has felt that.* Retrieved July 7, 2020, from Refinery 29: https://www.refinery29.com/en-ca/2020/07/9871564/mentorship-women-of-colour-media.

Arboine, N. (2020, September 2). *I'm a Black journalist in the UK. That simple fact still makes me unusual.* Retrieved from The Guardian: https://www.theguardian.com/commentisfree/2020/sep/02/black-journalist-uk-media-diversity-white.

Bailey, I. (2020, May 29). *George Floyd, Ahmaud Arbery, and one journalist's painfully honest self-examination on racism.* Retrieved August 8, 2020, from Nieman Reports: https://niemanreports.org/articles/george-floyd-ahmaud-arbery-and-one-journalists-painfully-honest-self-examination-on-racism/.

Balkissoon, D. (2020, June 17). *I tried to talk to my bosses about racism at work.* Retrieved July 5, 2020, from Chatelaine: https://www.chatelaine.com/opinion/racism-at-work/.

Batchelor-Hunt, N. (2020, June 4). *The British media needs to recognise Black Lives Matter as much as Madeleine McCann's.* Retrieved from Huffington Post UK: https://www.huffingtonpost.co.uk/entry/madeleine-mccann_uk_5ed8f1cdc5b6d561066181c7.

Batchelor-Hunt, N., & Walawakar, A. (2020, September 2). *'I could speak more freely': The enduring need for Black British media.* Retrieved from Each Other: https://eachother.org.uk/i-could-speak-more-freely-the-enduring-need-for-black-british-media/.

Belton, D. C. (2020, May 29). *Black journalists and covering the storm that never passes.* Retrieved June 30, 2020, from The Root: https://www.theroot.com/black-journalists-and-covering-the-storm-that-never-pas-1843756825.

Bennett, D. (2020, September 19). *The reality and the hope.* Retrieved October 8, 2020, from Sportsnet: https://www.sportsnet.ca/more/facing-sports-medias-damaging-lack-diversity/.

Berger, A. A. (2000). *Media and communication research methods: An introduction to qualitative and quantitative approaches.* Thousand Oaks, CA: Sage.

Braxton, G. (2020, September 27). *A Black reporter recalls racism in the newsroom and finally gets his day of reckoning.* Retrieved October 8, 2020, from Los Angeles Times: https://www.latimes.com/opinion/story/2020-09-27/black-reporter-racism-los-angeles-times-newsroom.

Byerly, C. M., & Wilson, C. C. (2009). Journalism as Kerner turns 40: Its multicultural problems and possibilities. *The Howard Journal of Communications, 20,* 209–221.

Callison, C., & Young, M. L. (2020). *Reckoning: Journalism's limits and possibilities.* New York: Oxford University Press.

Campbell, M. (2020, June 11). *Black Canadian voices are more visible now than ever — but will corporations act before this month's motivation wanes?* Retrieved August 14, 2020, from Toronto Star: https://www.thestar.com/opinion/contributors/2020/06/11/black-canadian-journalists-are-more-visible-now-than-ever-but-will-decision-makers-still-be-amplifying-their-voices-a-month-from-now.html.

Clark, B. (2014a, October 17). "Walking up a down-escalator": the interplay between newsroom norms and media coverage of. *In Media, 5.* Retrieved from http://inmedia.revues.org/749.

Clark, B. (2014b). Framing Canada's Aborignal Peoples: A comparative analysis of Indigenous and mainstream television news. *Canadian Journal of Native Studies, 34*(2), 41–64.

Crenshaw, K. (1997). Intersectionality and identity politics: Learning from violence against women of color. In M. L. Shanley, & N. U (Eds.), *Reconstructing political theory: Feminist perspectives* (pp. 178–193). State College, PA: Pennsylvania State University Press.

Dilday, E. (2020, September 16). *Journalists can help people tell their own stories by talking less, listening more.* Retrieved October 8, 2020, from Nieman Reports: https://niemanreports.org/articles/journalists-can-help-people-tell-their-own-stories-by-talking-less-listening-more/.

Douglas, D. (2020, July 14). *Meet the new black press.* Retrieved from Nieman Reports: https://niemanreports.org/articles/meet-the-new-black-press/.

Elian, M. B. (2020, July 29). *In photographing social justice protests, respect means 'looking again'.* Retrieved September 21, 2020, from Nieman Reports: https://niemanreports.org/articles/in-photographing-social-justice-protests-respect-means-looking-again/.

Fowler, M., & Pulfer, R. (2020, June 23). *It's time to bring more Indigenous voices into newsrooms.* Retrieved November 11, 2020, from The Globe and Mail: https://www.theglobeandmail.com/opinion/article-its-time-to-bring-more-indigenous-voices-into-newsrooms/.

Genier, C. (2020, June 8). *Thank you to everyone who has reached out. This is my statement.* Retrieved July 13, 2020, from Facebook: https://m.facebook.com/nt/screen/?params=%7B%22note_id%22%3A278129326755736%7D&path=%2Fnotes%2F%7Bnote_id%7D&_rdr.

Gillespie, E. (2020, August 17). *Karl Stefanovic under fire after comments on media diversity report.* Retrieved from SBS News: https://www.sbs.com.au/news/the-feed/karl-stefanovic-under-fire-after-comments-on-media-diversity-report.

Haltiwanger, J. (2020, September 11). *Twitter users dunk on the New York Times' Paul Krugman after he said 9/11 didn't lead to a 'mass outbreak' of Islamophobia or violence.* Retrieved from Business Insider: https://www.businessinsider.com/twitter-paul-krugman-new-york-times-backlash-911-tweets-2020-9.

Harewood, A. (2020, June 26). *Fighting For Our Vision, Together.* Retrieved September 30, 2020, from Canadian Media Guild: https://webcache.googleusercontent.com/search?q=cache:EILm2lpPMesJ:https://www.cmg.

ca/en/2020/06/26/fighting-for-our-vision-together-2/+&cd=1&hl=en&ct=
clnk&gl=ca.

Hickmon, G. (2020, September 4). *To build an anti-racist media, look to BI-
POC communities.* Retrieved October 1, 2020, from studyhall.xyz: https://
studyhall.xyz/to-build-an-anti-racist-media-look-to-bipoc-communities/

Hong, J. (2020, June 17). *Yukon Morning hosts resigns over suppression of
Black, Indigenous voices at CBC.* Retrieved July 7, 2020, from Yukon News:
https://www.yukon-news.com/news/yukon-morning-hosts-resigns-over-
suppression-of-black-indigenous-voices-at-cbc/.

Insiders ABC. (2020, June 13). Retrieved from Twitter: https://twitter.
com/InsidersABC/status/1271944249030803456?ref_src=twsrc%5Etf-
w%7Ctwcamp%5Etweetembed%7Ctwterm%5E1271944249030803456%
7Ctwgr%5E%7Ctwcon%5Es1_&ref_url=https%3A%2F%2Fwww.the-
guardian.com%2Fmedia%2F2020%2Fjun%2F28%2Fit-dampens-the-
conversation-n.

Jackson, S. J. (2020, June 3). *The headlines that are covering up police
violence.* Retrieved October 8, 2020, from The Atlantic: https://www.
theatlantic.com/culture/archive/2020/06/george-floyd-protests-what-news-
reports-dont-say/612571/.

Jones, K., & Okun, T. (2001). *The characteristics of white supremacy culture.*
Retrieved from Showing Up For Racial Justice: https://www.showingupfor-
racialjustice.org/white-supremacy-culture-characteristics.html.

Jones, S. (2020, June 9). *I'm The Inquirer's only black male news columnist.
That speaks to a larger problem.* Retrieved July 7, 2020, from inquirer.com:
https://www.inquirer.com/opinion/racism-media-black-reporters-editors-
philadelphia-inquirer-pittsburgh-20200609.html.

Kendi, I. X. (2016). *Stamped form the beginning: The definitve history of racist
ideas in America.* New York: Nation Books.

King, R. (2020, September 22). *Journalists need to create a sense of belonging.*
Retrieved October 18, 2020, from Nieman Reports: https://niemanreports.
org/articles/journalists-need-to-create-a-sense-of-belonging/.

Lowery, W. (2020, June 23). *A reckoning over objectivity, led by Black journalists.* Retrieved July 7, 2020, from The New York Times: https://www.nytimes.
com/2020/06/23/opinion/objectivity-black-journalists-coronavirus.html.

Mattar, P. (2020, August 21). *Objectivity is a privilege afforded to white journalists.* Retrieved September 1, 2020, from The Walrus: https://thewalrus.ca/
objectivity-is-a-privilege-afforded-to-white-journalists/.

Melan Mag. (2020, July 4). *The Black industry groups making BLM a movement
not a moment.* Retrieved from Melan Mag: https://melanmag.com/2020/07/04/
the-black-industry-groups-making-blm-a-movement-not-a-moment/.

Miller, E. (2020, September 1). *How two local newsrooms are sewing diversity
into the fabric of their organizations.* Retrieved from Poynter: https://www.
poynter.org/business-work/2020/how-two-local-newsrooms-are-sewing-
diversity-into-the-fabric-of-their-organizations/.

National Advisory Commission on Civil Disorders. (1968). *The Report of the
National Advisory Commission on Civil Disorders.* New York: New York
Times Publications.

Newman-Bremang, K. (2020, July 7). *For black women in media, a "dream job" is a myth.* Retrieved August 14, 2020, from Refinery 29: https://www. refinery29.com/en-ca/2020/07/9878117/systemic-racism-canadian-media.

Pierre-Louis, K. (2020, June 24). *It's time to change the way the media reports on protests. Here are some ideas.* Retrieved October 31, 2020, from Nieman-Lab: https://www.niemanlab.org/2020/06/its-time-to-change-the-way-the-media-reports-on-protests-here-are-some-ideas/.

Potts, T. (2020, June 22). *Journalists of color are part of the story of racism in America. That raises tough questions on the job.* Retrieved September 14, 2020, from Center for Health Journalism: https://centerforhealthjournalism. org/2020/06/19/journalists-color-are-part-story-racism-america-raises-tough-questions-job.

Prior, L. (2014). Content analysis. In P. Leavy (Ed.), *The Oxford handbook of qualitative research* (pp. 359–379). New York: Oxford University Press.

Rice, W. (2020, August 31). *Letter to a Young Indigenous Journalist.* Retrieved September 7, 2020, from The Walrus: https://thewalrus.ca/terra-cognita-letter-to-a-young-indigenous-journalist/.

Roache, T. (2020, September 24). *#278 Lobster Politics.* Retrieved from canadaland.com: https://www.canadaland.com/podcast/278-lobster-politics/.

Rudhran, M. (2020, May 23). *What it's really like being Black in white spaces.* Retrieved from Syrup: https://www.syrupaus.com/news-politics/being-black-in-white-spaces-bittersweet-podcast/.

Said, E. (1978/2003). *Orientalism.* London: Penguin Books.

Smith, B. (2020, June 7). *The media equation: inside the revolts erupting in america's big newsrooms.* Retrieved July 13, 2020, from nytimes.com: https://www.nytimes.com/2020/06/07/business/media/new-york-times-washington-post-protests.html.

Staples, B. (2020, June 4). Retrieved August 8, 2020, from Twitter: https:// twitter.com/BrentNYT/status/1268541141416325121.

Stewart, B. (2016). Twitter as method: Using Twitter as a tool to conduct research. In L. Sloan, & A. Quan-Haase (Eds.), *The SAGE handbook of social media research methods* (pp. 251–263). Sage Publications.

Troian, M. (2020, May 31). Retrieved from Twitter: https://twitter.com/ozhibiiige/status/1256402841184473089.

Truong, D. (2020, June 5). *Dear newsroom managers, journalists of color can't do all the work.* Retrieved August 8, 2020, from Poynter: https://www.poynter.org/ethics-trust/2020/dear-newsroom-managers-journalists-of-color-cant-do-all-the-work/.

White, N. (2020a, August 28). *Exclusive: BBC staff accuse corporation of being 'institutionally racist'.* Retrieved from Huffington Post UK: https:// www.huffingtonpost.co.uk/amp/entry/bbc-institutionally-racist_uk_ 5f3f9c78c5b697824f977779/?__twitter_impression=true&guccounter=2&-guce_referrer=aHR0cHM6Ly93d3cudGhlZ3VhcmRpYW4uY29tL2Nvb-W1lbnRpc2ZyZWUvMjAyMC9zZXAvMDIvYmxhY2stam91cm5hbGlzd-CllaytZWR.

White, N. (2020b, August 29). *Exclusive: Black BBC staff morale at 'All time low' after N-word scandal.* Retrieved from Huffington Post UK:

https://www.huffingtonpost.co.uk/entry/bbc-n-word-staff-morale-low_uk_5f43f0a8c5b66a80ee1621f6.

Zhou, N. (2020, June 28). *'It dampens the conversation': no more excuses for Australian media's lack of diversity.* Retrieved from The Guardian: https://www.theguardian.com/media/2020/jun/28/it-dampens-the-conversation-no-more-excuses-for-australian-medias-lack-of-diversity.

3 'Twas Always Thus
Systemic Racism, Newsgathering, and Content

Introduction

Based on the media accounts from Indigenous and racialized journalists in Chapter 2, this chapter traces the research on the news media and race over the last 50 years, specifically the impact of systemic racism on news production and content. That research details the mis- and under-reporting of racialized groups and Indigenous Peoples, corroborating the concerns raised by journalists in the previous chapter. The chapter extends the classic ethnographic studies of the past (Gans, Tuchman, Tunstall, Fishman), that underscored white hegemony and white privilege in news production norms, to newsgathering in the 21st century. Two cases from 2020 serve to illustrate the existing and emerging scholarship: A Black photojournalist's approach to covering Black Lives Matter (BLM) protests in New York, and false balance and missing historical context in news reports on the Mi'kmaw lobster fishery on Canada's Atlantic coast. Additional discussion contrasts Black and Indigenous media with mainstream news, revealing the dominant white bias that shapes most news content. The comparison illustrates the importance of shifting the media gaze from a dominant, white perspective to one that is inclusive, resulting in a more equitable and accurate media discourse. In fact, many of the reforms called for through the racial reckoning are well-established in the newsgathering practices of ethnic and Indigenous news media.

Power, Colonialism, and Mainstream Media

Journalism, like all institutions in Western society, is the product of colonialism, patriarchy, power, and racial exclusion. Any examination of news norms and news content must start with understanding how those forces are at work in gatekeeping, agenda-setting, and framing.

DOI: 10.4324/9781003261544-4

Who decides what is and is not news? Who chooses the issues and events that must be covered in the public interest? Who determines the voices that will appear in the news discourse, and which ones will be left out? Who decides what is salient to the discussion and what can or should be ignored? In most cases, the answer to all these questions has been predominantly white men. This is borne out in news media diversity surveys in the United States, Australia, Canada, Europe, and the United Kingdom that continue to show disproportionally higher participations rates for white men as both journalists and managers (see Malik & Fatah, 2019; News Leaders Association, 2019; Arvanitakis et al., 2020; Papper, 2020; Women in Journalism, 2020; Canadian Association of Journalists, 2021).

There can be little doubt that Western societies are based on "interlocking systems that work together to uphold and maintain cultures of domination," systems that bell hooks (2013) describes as the "imperialist white supremacist capitalist patriarchy" (p. 4). The political class is overwhelmingly white: 78 per cent of US Congress (Bialik, 2019), 89 per cent of Canadian political leaders (Grenier, 2020), 90 per cent of Members of Parliament in the British House of Commons (Uberoi & Lees, 2020). There have only been 11 Black, eight Asian, and three Native Americans elected to the US senate over its entire history (United States Senate, 2021). White dominance manifests similarly in corporate leadership, where 81 per cent of executives and board members in Fortune 500 companies are white (DeHaas, Akutagawa, & Spriggs, 2019).

The white, Eurocentric, patriarchal vision of the world exists at the heart of all systems of meaning, governance, communication and commerce, a worldview shaped by 500 years of colonialism. In his seminal work, *Orientalism*, Said (1978/2003), describes how Western consciousness understands the "Orient" – what could also be broadly interpreted as the world outside Europe and its colonies – as subordinate to the "Occident" in every respect. Europe is a "collective notion," he writes:

> …identifying "us" Europeans against all "those" non-Europeans, and indeed it can be argued that the major component in European culture is precisely what makes hegemonic both inside and outside Europe: the idea of European identity as a superior one in comparison with all the non-European peoples and cultures. (p. 7)

Orientalism, Said suggests, is driven by the cultural hegemony described by Antonio Gramsci, whereby the perceptions of the dominant economic class are spread through society by media institutions in concert with the church, families, and universities, assuring those values came "to be accepted as being for the general good" (McNair, 1998, p. 27). Power is reflected in the social binaries that come to define the dominant class from the subordinate, Occident versus Orient, "us" versus "them," civilized versus backwards. Hall (1997) explains that power binary in representations of race, whereby society understands "Black" by its contrast to "white," arguing that it is "the *'difference'* between *white* and *black* which signifies, which carries meaning" (p. 234, italics in the original). Hall references Derrida in noting that one side of the binary is typically "the dominant one," and that there is always a power relation between the two (p. 235). Power binaries turn up in news media discourse all the time, as white/Black, settler/"Indian," civilized/savage, police/protester, citizen/immigrant (Clark, 2014).

Colonialism and cultural hegemony explain the editorial gatekeeping and "story angles" pursued by mainstream newsrooms, captured in Robert Entman's (1993) interpretation of framing theory. Entman describes the process by which journalists shape their coverage as selecting "some aspects of a perceived reality" and then making them "more salient in a communicating text, in such a way as to promote a particular problem definition, causal interpretation, moral evaluation, and/or treatment recommendation" (p. 52). He maintains that the news frame is the result of "actors of interest" competing to "dominate the text" and thus the frame is "really the imprint of power" (p. 55). Although there can be "independent framing" offering interpretations outside the hegemony model, Entman suggests mainstream media tend to "exhibit homogenous framing" (p. 55), privileging dominant voices over the marginalized, allowing for coverage that is stereotypic, sensational, and lacking full context, such as police discrimination and violence, inner-city poverty, and chronic unemployment (Entman & Rojecki, 2001, p. 49). Whiteness defines the frame, as Hall (1990) points out, "The 'white eye' is always outside the frame – but seeing and positioning everything within it" (p. 14, cited in Tolley, 2016, p. 182).

Production Norms, Objectivity, and White Dominance

White dominance is deeply entrenched in production norms and professional ethics. Classic studies of news practice have long detailed the contradictions inherent in notions of journalistic objectivity, especially as it relates to privilege, power, and race. Shoemaker and Reese (1996) make the connection between elites and established newsgathering norms that "must conform to hegemonic requirements" (p. 235). They argue the "notion of objectivity" is fundamental in establishing whose voices are newsworthy and important, and whose are not. This is especially significant in discussions of newsroom diversity and reporting on race, giving rise to the situation where journalists are accused of being "biased when they use their own expertise to draw conclusions... [but] objective when they let prominent sources dictate the news" (p. 235). A number of journalism scholars, most notably Jay Rosen, have incorporated Thomas Nagel's description of objectivity as "the view from nowhere." Rosen contends that such a conceptualization serves as a middle ground for partisan politics and polarizing issues, and a defense against bias (Rosen, 2010). Bias is the antithesis of objectivity, and in a racial context, used as a "code for difference" by journalists (Callison & Young, 2020, p. 11). Over the years, there has been sufficient ambivalence regarding objectivity that many professional associations have dropped the term from their codes of ethics, including the Society of Professional Journalists (Wallace, 2019, p. 7). However, despite some recognition of the profound contradictions in "journalism's dominant authority" from scholars and practitioners alike, "the vast majority [of journalists] have not gone far enough in understanding how legitimizing a 'view from nowhere' impacts power relations both internal and external to the profession" (Callison & Young, 2020, p. 4). In other words, the objectivity ideal continues to dominate production norms and content. Given the over-representation of white staff in mainstream newsrooms, objectivity is practiced and enforced – not as view from nowhere – but through a lens of white, male dominance and privilege, a common refrain from journalists of color through the racial reckoning.

In most newsrooms, a story is not a story until it has been "confirmed" by official sources, people who are in positions of authority, typically white men, and seen as "knowers" (Fishman, 1980, p. 56). Shoemaker and Reese suggest that to do otherwise, to draw on the "nonofficial" voices of ordinary people or the marginalized, "is discouraged as unnewsworthy. By accepting valueless reporting [objectivity] as the norm, the media accept the boundaries, values and ideological rules of the game established and interpreted by elite sources" (p. 235). Gans (1979) argues this reliance on official sources also stems from the fact that "the most powerful sources are also the most efficient," which further adds to their power (p. 282). As a result, journalists are constantly accessing institutions where they can easily connect with powerful voices: parliaments, legislatures, city halls, courtrooms, police stations, universities, corporate news conferences, so that "the story of journalism, on a day-to-day basis, is the story of the interaction of reporters and officials" (Schudson, 1989, p. 271). Ericson, Baranek and Chan (1989), in their study of interactions between news sources and reporters in Canada, conclude "news represents *who* are the authorized knowers and *what* are their authoritative versions of reality" (p. 3, italics in the original). "Knowers" shape the newsgathering routines with "phase structures" such as media availabilities or news conferences in which organizations showcase their knowers to provide "specific schemes of interpretation" (Fishman, 1980, p. 55). Without phase structures, reporters must work harder to find sources recognized for their legitimacy.

Given the predominance of white people in positions of authority, newsgathering norms tend to filter out the voices and perspectives of Indigenous Peoples, people of color, and marginalized groups. In fact, the scholarship shows between the application of objectivity and established routines of practice, mainstream journalism privileges white narratives, and mirrors the systemic racism in wider society.

Patterns of Misrepresentation and the White Newsroom

Over the last four decades, study after study in Western countries has found racialized, Indigenous, and immigrant communities are typically under-represented and negatively portrayed in mainstream news coverage (van Dijk, 1991; Teo, 2000; Pease, Smith, & Subervi, 2001; Henry & Tator, 2002; Downing & Husband, 2005; Jenkins, 2012; LeDuff, 2012; Wilson, Gutierrez, & Chao, 2013; Bishop, 2016; Callison & Young, 2020). Blacks are more likely to appear in the news discourse in association with crime, but much less likely as experts (Entman, 1994; Wilson & Gutierrez, 1995; Entman & Rojecki, 2001; Campbell et al., 2012). White faces and voices dominate the mainstream media content, but when racialized groups do make the news, representations of Blacks, LatinX, and Asians can lack context, tend to the episodic, and disproportionately negative (Pease, Smith, & Subervi, 2001, p. 2). Similarly, refugees and racialized newcomers are frequently cast as threats to the dominant order, and immigration is couched in fearful language, such as a "crime wave or invasion...framed metaphorically as a dangerous pollutant" (Cisneros, 2008, p. 578, cited in Bishop, 2016, p. 146). Muslims and Sikhs are depicted as "militants" and "terrorists," potentially engaged in "illegal activity" (Henry & Tator, 2002, p. 137).

Callison and Young (2020) have noted an increase in the reporting of Indigenous issues in Canada but acknowledge "more coverage doesn't mean good or appropriate coverage" (p. 165). They say mainstream news content has "reflected a deficit model where Indigenous people are represented as less than the mainstream public, degenerate, in conflict, and/or unable to manage their own affairs." Anishinaabe journalist Duncan McCue, creator of the website Reporting in Indigenous Communities, recounts a simple rule of stereotypes he learned from an elder: "the only way an Indian would make it on the news is if he or she is one of the four Ds, drumming, dancing, drunk or dead" (McCue, 2021). Those tropes are captured in studies that show the news media's predilection to incorporate the colonial binary, framing First Nations as "others," distinct from the rest of the country (Harding, 2006; Anderson & Robertson, 2011; Chow-White & McMahon, 2011). Researchers have examined news coverage related to land claims, treaty disputes, protests and blockades, finding a reliance on "wartime characterizations" that assert the "social dichotomy of us against them that has persisted since the colonial era" (Lambertus, 2004, p. 200), and portray Indigenous "collective actors" as "criminals, threats to peaceful race relations, and expensive" (Wilkes, Corrigall-Brown, & Ricard, 2010, p. 54). Scholarship in the United States (see Weston, 1996) and Australia arrive at similar findings. McCallum's (2007) analysis of Australian newspaper coverage of Indigenous Peoples concluded reporters most often focused on the sensational, "drawing on the news value of conflict... and narrating Indigenous peoples and issues as *problematic*" so that "Indigenous men are framed as *dangerous others*" and ultimately pose a *"threat to the existing order"* (p. 12, italics in the original).

As noted above, inequitable news coverage is the product of colonialism and cultural hegemony, which in turn shaped journalism's production norms and ethical codes. White supremacy similarly manifests as newsrooms staffed by predominantly white journalists, especially in senior positions. This further ensures the creation of news content that leans heavily toward the dominant, white perspective. Schudson identifies the impact as a bias "toward people who look like the majority of journalists over people who do not" (2011, p. 54). He quotes a Black journalist, Vanessa Williams of *The Washington Post*, explaining how the murder of a white person receives more media attention than the killing of an African-American because of the racial make-up of news staff: "the people who make decisions about what is newsworthy more readily identify with victims who look like them and live like them and are utterly frightened or outraged when bad things happen to them" (p. 54). While the numbers of racialized and Indigenous reporters in the industry continues to grow, they struggle to address this double standard, as described through the racial reckoning and in Chapter 2, but also captured in earlier studies. An analysis of Black and LatinX journalists in the United States finds when they try to bring their personal insights on racial issues into the newsroom they might be accused of being biased, "being labeled unprofessional" and ought to "'act' like journalists, not like minorities" (Nishikawa, Towner, Clawson, & Waltenburg, 2009, pp. 245, 250). Another analysis describes how racialized news staff find their input into editorial decision-making is "often disregarded because white colleagues define news" from their own white lens on the world (Wilson, Gutierrez, & Chao, 2013, p. 128). A study from Canada examined newsgathering at a CBC station and highlighted the tendency of typically white, middle-class producers to "frame coverage from that dominant perspective" (Clark, 2014, p. 13). It is not surprising, therefore, that scholars of news production assert that "persons of color [need to] occupy critical positions of power" to challenge "racist traditions and patterns" in news practice, and deliver more equitable coverage (Johnston & Flamiano, 2007, p. 111). Tolley (2016) frames the discussion from the perspective of white news staff, who do not recognize their complicity in "racialized coverage" because they "do not acknowledge how deeply ingrained racial assumptions and institutional whiteness affect news coverage" (p. 185).

Over the years, the scholarship related to race and journalism identified many instances where the white supremacy that imbues newsgathering norms as described in this chapter led to issues of under- and misrepresentation of marginalized groups. While some have argued those cases are in the past, and journalism today is much more inclusive, the racial reckoning demonstrated in some respects how little has changed. There is no shortage of examples to choose from. What follows are two cases where the findings of news and race scholars described in this chapter manifest in familiar patterns of othering racialized and Indigenous peoples, privileging white voices, and downplaying systemic racism. There were other stories that garnered more headlines and attention, but these two demonstrate how easily newsgathering falls into the same routines of practice that fail under-represented communities.

Lobster Fishery Coverage

Many people outside of Canada's Atlantic coast will not be very familiar with the seafood industry and its history with Indigenous fishing rights. Surprisingly, neither were mainstream news organizations when non-Indigenous fishermen started harassing Mi'kmaw lobster boats, crews, and customers in the fall of 2020. That is when the Sipekne'katik First Nation launched a "moderate livelihood" lobster fishery, outside the non-Indigenous season. In 1999, the Supreme Court of Canada affirmed the Mi'kmaw treaty rights to hunt, fish and gather, in a famous case involving Mi'kmaw fisher Donald Marshall, who had caught and sold about 500 pounds of eels for just under $800. The court based its ruling on the Peace and Friendship Treaties of 1752, 1760 and 1761 (Leonard, 2020). Non-Indigenous fishers said they were concerned the Mi'kmaw fishery would cause irreparable damage to stocks, but the Mi'kmaw fishery pointed out the vast difference in scale between their 350 traps compared to the 390,000 deployed in the commercial fishery. When the Sipekne'katik set out to drop their traps in St. Mary's Bay, non-Indigenous fishers pursued in their own boats, shouting threats, and firing flares at them. On land they vandalized Mi'kmaw traps, confronted the Indigenous lobster fishers bringing in their catch, and set fire to a lobster pound, destroying much the structure and the Mi'kmaw harvest, an estimated $3 million in damage (Canadian Press, 2020).

However, while the non-Indigenous fishers were the ones protesting, harassing, and vandalizing, mainstream coverage generally represented the situation as a dispute, as "a two-party conflict with two sides, as about being about conservation and equality – when all of that misses the mark," according to Mi'kmaw lawyer Pam Palmater, who holds the chair in Indigenous Governance at Ryerson University in Toronto (Leonard, 2020). She points out the size of the Mi'kmaw lobster fishery is "a fraction" of one per cent of the total commercial catch, representing no threat to the lobster stocks, a fact often overlooked in the news coverage. There were not two sides attacking each other, and so the accurate framing, Palmater suggests, "would be non-native Nova Scotia fishermen have escalated their racism, violence, intimidation tactics, and criminality against Mi'kmaw and local businesses to stop them from fishing."

Others demonstrated how mainstream news coverage missed important historic and legal context. The Canadaland podcast offered examples from television reports, including one where a journalist described the Indigenous fishery as being "in defiance of federal regulations that say the fishery is closed for the season" (Brown, 2020), when that policy does not apply to the Sipekne'katik fishers. Another TV report sought to attribute what is fact as a Mi'kmaw opinion, declaring the Mi'kmaq "*say* a supreme court ruling grants them the right to catch and sell lobster outside the regular lobster season (italics added)"

(CBC News, 2020). It is not conjecture or opinion, the Mi'kmaq do have that right as confirmed by the high court in 1999, and reaffirmed again at the height of the non-Indigenous attacks in 2020 by the Supreme Court of Nova Scotia when the Sipekne'katik sought and were granted an injunction to prevent anyone from interfering with their fishing activities (Canadian Press, 2020). In another instance of misreporting, a CBC online news story used the word "illegal" in a headline to describe lobster traps associated with the Mi'kmaw fishery, but later changed it when it was pointed out the Mi'kmaq have a treaty right to fish (Brown, 2020).

As the study in Chapter 2 found, the white normative view associated with news media manifests as ignorance of racialized or Indigenous history and experience, resulting in a critical lack of context. Reporters who were unfamiliar with treaty law and the Marshall decision reported on the concerns of non-Indigenous fishers without providing that vital background – perhaps the most significant information – to their audiences. Initially, there were not a lot of mainstream news resources dedicated to the story, and it was not until Indigenous media started to challenge some of the mainstream narratives that news coverage started to improve. Trina Roache, a Mi'kmaw video-journalist at the Aboriginal Peoples Television Network, in an interview with CBC, described the ways news organizations had misrepresented the story:

> ...we sort of assume that somehow mainstream journalism, predominantly white journalism, that is just sort of unbiased... Because I've been asked, well, how do you keep your journalism from turning into advocacy? And I'm like, that's a terrible question, because you're making an assumption somehow that because I'm Mi'kmaq reporting on Mi'kmaw issues that I can't be fair and accurate and balanced. And instead, when CBC or other media are calling this fishery an illegal fishery or keep referring to it within the report as this illegal fishery, to me that's bias, right? That betrays an inherent bias in the reporting and not including enough Mi'kmaw voices.
>
> CBC News (2020)

Photojournalism and a Brooklyn BLM protest

Photojournalism can often become a flashpoint for criticism related to controversial news stories. It also provides a distinct and effective way to consider the forces that shape news discourse, a form of representation overshadowed by discussions of word-choice and head-lines, but with the power to convey so much meaning in the time it takes to open a newspaper or open a link on Facebook. In the data set under analysis in the previous chapter, an article by Melissa Bunni Elian in *Nieman Reports* focuses specifically on visual communication and its role in stereotyping or otherwise misrepresenting racialized groups. It was her work that referenced the experiences of photojour-nalist David "Dee" Delgado as he interacted with BLM demonstra-tors and white photographers in New York, as described in Chapter 2. Delgado recalled seeing a man who was intoxicated and angry, per-haps out for revenge, but someone he saw as "a guy that's hurt, and he has no other way to vocalize that hurt but with rage" (Elian, 2020). However, a white photojournalist observed, "there goes an instigator," a comment that was "burned" in Delgado's memory. According to Delgado, white photographers started "photographing him angry and trying to antagonize the crowd," likely capturing stereotypic, threat-ening images of Black aggression and conflict. Rather than focusing on this one troubled individual – "looking for the anarchy" – Delgado documented the real story, the response of the crowd, "calming him down and talking to him and telling him that that wasn't the way." One of his pictures shows the man gesturing angrily while a fellow demonstrator puts an arm around his shoulders, and another puts his hands on his waist, clear attempts to comfort the man. His unchecked emotion is still captured in the image, but the inaccurate trope of the angry mob and related chaos is replaced by a much more authentic visual narrative.

Elian advocates photojournalists adopt an approach based on sys-tems dynamics, "the study of the interconnectedness of life," which calls for a "continuous view" of events, issues, and problems. She notes that "the news media's emphasis on conflict is part of a feed-back loop that maintains stereotypes about the Black experience in America," but that racialized photojournalists "are acutely aware of this dynamic and often create work to counter narrow and incomplete narratives" (Elian, 2020). Delgado's story of the BLM protester is a prime example.

Delgado's experiences are corroborated in a study of the photojour-nalism during the race-related University of Missouri protests in 2015, which finds white photographers tend to follow "scripts" associated with familiar, "dominant" narratives (Thomson, 2016). The photo-journalists interviewed suggested they were aware of established sto-rylines, representing protesters as angry, "irrational, unreasonable," but said what they primarily look for are subjects who are "expressive"

(p. 227). They also described concentrating on the "important sub-jects," the people who seemed to be the leaders, looking for cues such as megaphones to determine who those people are. Moreover, as a group, they acknowledged taking an "outsiders" approach to captur-ing the event and admitted "they had low or no familiarity with people of color and race-related issues" (p. 226). According to the researcher, the resulting images tended to focus on the prominent participants of what was really a grassroots event, and dominated by Black protest-ers, when there was significant participation by white people, conclud-ing that "Multiracial portrayals lessen the likelihood that journalists adopt an 'us versus them' frame and are more likely to resonate with an audience" (p. 229).

The issues raised by the University of Missouri study and Delgado's story offer lessons for more inclusive photojournalism, but also more inclusive reporting generally, and are consistent with the findings from the analysis in Chapter 2. The white photojournalists in Delgado's case could be thought of as outsiders just as the photographers saw themselves in the U of M analysis, approaching the story of protest with the same objective orthodoxy shown to be a "white normative view" through the racial reckoning. The fact that the white photojour-nalist in Brooklyn could not see past the rage of the man he labeled an "instigator," could not empathize with his despair, suggests a lack of understanding of the racial experience, something the Missouri pho-tographers openly confessed to as well. Without that knowledge – at a personal or institutional level – newsrooms are prone to missteps such as the "Send in the Troops" or "Buildings Matter, Too" editori-als. More nuanced images, such as Delgado's photo of the protester being embraced and consoled by two others, moves beyond tropes of conflict and violence, the familiar casting of non-whites as "problem people." As columnist Solomon Jones noted in the previous chapter, news media need to treat "African Americans as human beings with stories to be told rather than characters with drama to be exploited" (Jones, 2020). Elian takes it back to the lens of photojournalism:

> When photographing protracted struggles, the story can't always be told in the heat of the moment. When our images are myopic, so is the overall framing of our news stories. Similar to a camera's lenses, the frameworks we use in our work must be interchangeable.
>
> Elian (2020)

The analogy extends to all aspects of newsgathering. As these two case studies from the racial reckoning demonstrate, racial myopia in news media, to extend Elian's analysis, is challenged when there are empowered, non-white news staff on board. In the case of the Mi'kmaw lobster fishery, Indigenous journalists were the ones correcting the false-balanced frames of mainstream news media. The example from the Brooklyn BLM protest shows how a Black Puerto Rican photojournalist adds depth of understanding and context his white counterparts might not recognize. A Black perspective on demonstrations against discrimination, or an Indigenous perspective on Treaty rights, is central to these stories. The failure of mainstream news media to properly include these perspectives opens the door for so-called ethnic and Indigenous media to fill the void. The next section looks at how those news organizations do that and what mainstream news outlets could learn from them.

Black and Indigenous Media

Indigenous, diasporic, ethnic, and Black news media have been longtime fixtures in the mediascape of most Western countries. Typically, they are enterprises staffed and controlled by members of the ethnic group for which the content is intended. Studies have shown that these news organizations enjoy a significant readership and are preferred over mainstream media by 45 per cent of the racialized audience according to one analysis (Bendixen & Associates, 2005, p. 8). Regardless of the intended consumer, ethnic media exist due to the "continuing under-/misrepresentation of ethnoracial minorities in mainstream media employment and content" (Yu, 2019, p. 67). In other words, the inability of mainstream news organizations to provide the content sought by racialized and Indigenous audiences, and the fact that those newsrooms hire disproportionally fewer journalists from those groups, has created demand for ethnic alternatives. Studies have shown Black, LatinX, Indigenous, and diasporic media in North America and around the world are more inclusive of non-white voices and focus their coverage on issues important to their communities (Georgiou, 2005; Deuze, 2006; Wilson, Gutierrez, & Chao, 2013; Lopez, 2013; Clark, 2014; Gomez-Aguinaga, 2021).

A comparative analysis of mainstream television news with Indigenous news coverage in Canada demonstrates the value of inclusive newsrooms (Clark, 2014). Framing analysis was used to examine the differences in the way stories on Indigenous issues/events were presented by mainstream national networks – CBC, Global News, and CTV – with content on those same issues/events by the Aborignal Peoples Television Network (APTN), an Indigenous broadcaster. The qualitative study revealed – not surprisingly – a tendency on the part of mainstream news to "frame Indigenous people in a stereotypic pattern consistent with a Eurocentric, colonial lens" while APTN was more likely to include Indigenous context and "challenge the colonial stereotypes" offering more accurate coverage of Indigenous communities (Clark, 2014, p. 42). There were times when the non-Indigenous media did include proper context and Indigenous perspectives, but not consistently. One case from the study examined news coverage of an airline pulling its flight crews out of a downtown hotel in Winnipeg over safety concerns about displaced flood evacuees being temporarily housed in the area, complaining there had been incidents of "public intoxication" and "crimes of violence." Those evacuees were all residents of First Nations communities though the airline never mentioned this in its original, leaked memo, which triggered the news coverage. In their coverage of the story, none of the mainstream news networks interviewed a single evacuee; APTN's story – produced by an Indigenous journalist – included several of the displaced First Nation citizens (p. 52). In a rather egregious use of stereotypic imagery, CTV's piece opened with footage of two intoxicated, Indigenous men panhandling, individuals who were clearly not evacuees and had no connection to the story, beyond simply being Indigenous. Indigenous new staff at APTN would have recognized that framing as racist and avoided it. Moreover, their mandate to provide Indigenous perspectives ensured the story would never have gone to air without including the voices of the First Nations evacuees at the heart of the issue.

The difference between the mainstream coverage and APTN is decolonization. Indigenous media, and most forms of ethnic media, "challenge the frames of the dominant culture through self-representation, 'rendering visible Indigenous cultural and historical realities to themselves and the broader societies that have stereotyped or denied them'" (Ginsburg, 1994, p. 378, cited in Clark, 2014, pp. 45–46). Roth (2005) writes that Indigenous media operate outside the colonial, white settler lens that shapes mainstream news organizations; the creative control they have over news content allows them to tear down "antiquated power relations" (p. 220). Knopf (2010) suggests Indigenous media provide a decolonized alternative discourse by "creating self-determined images free of stereotypes and objectification" (p. 93), noting that at APTN the news operation focuses on issues facing Indigenous Peoples from an Indigenous perspective, asserting to the audience that "Aboriginal cultures do have rich cultural knowledge that is worth becoming familiar with," and challenging "Euro-Canadian" assumptions of inferiority (p. 95). The experience is the same in other parts of the world where Indigenous peoples seek to challenge the colonial narratives of settlers living around them. In

Aotearoa-New Zealand, Indigenous radio is well-established allowing "Indigenous nations [to] develop their own media and form media networks on their own terms," thereby reframing "what media mean in Indigenous contexts and according to indigenous discourses" (De Bruin & Mane, 2018, p. 128).

Taking control of the means of production and narrative also works for other marginalized groups. The award-winning documentary, *Disclosure*, which explores the lived experiences of transgender people in Hollywood, was produced by trans director Sam Feder with a mostly transgender crew. If a trans technician could not be found, a cisgender person was hired to mentor a transgender person in the role. Feder explained the importance of such an approach: "Every step of film-making is so deeply informed by every hand that touches it. Trans people are the experts in their own history and should be centered in their storytelling" (Lopez, 2020). The film has been hailed as an authentic representation of life for transgender people, avoiding the familiar monolithic and stereotypic depictions of trans life. Studies have shown that media portrayals of transgenderism are infrequent, and use "delegitimizing language" that undermine transgender political aims (Billard, 2016), an issue that could be addressed were more trans individuals involved in producing media narratives.

In North America, the need for alternatives to the dominant, white, colonial news discourse was evident early on in the United States, when economic expediency trumped morality on the issue of slavery. The counternarrative was initially provided by *Freedom's Journal*, the first African-American owned and operated newspaper launched in 1827 and published in New York. It is credited with founding the abolitionist movement, recognizing the need to offer alternative portrayals of Black people and perspectives on slavery. This is captured in an early editorial from the newspaper:

> Too long has the public been deceived by misrepresentations of things which concern us dearly. From the press and the pulpit we have suffered much by being incorrectly represented ... Such should know more of our actual condition, and of our efforts and feelings, in forming or advocating for plans for our amelioration.
>
> Jackson (2020)

The Black press has long been an important fixture in the US mediascape, a trusted source of information through decades of white-dominated mainstream news. Through the pandemic, Black media were the first to highlight the disproportionate impact of the virus on the health and economic wellbeing of racialized people (Alcazaren-Keeley,

2020). Publications such as the *Washington Informer,* "a multi-media news organization serving the African-American community in metropolitan Washington D.C.," focused on higher rates of infection, hospitalization, and death among African Americans, playing a crucial role "in chronicling the COVID-19 crisis for audiences of color, and holding institutions accountable in the aftermath of the pandemic." By contrast, media critics in the United Kingdom noted the racialized groups were also disproportionately affected by COVID, but British officials were not held to account to the same extent for the inequity, perhaps a reflection of the limited presence of ethnic media there, as well as the dearth of racialized reporters in mainstream news (Arboine, 2020).

The ethnic media paradigm offers significant insights into journalism informed by experiences, cultures, and perspectives outside the white normative lens. However, Fleras (2016) turns the concept back on itself by theorizing mainstream media *"as if* they were white ethnic media whose mediated images of peoples, migrants and minorities superimpose a pro-white preference over an anti-minority bias" (italics in the original, p. 23). The author does this to address a paradox in misrepresentation, the fact that news organizations still struggle to report equitably and contextually on marginalized groups, despite diversity and inclusion efforts. Fleras acknowledges there are limits to such theorizing but points out the inability of mainstream media to recognizes its pervasive whiteness:

> Denying its existence may have the effect of privileging whiteness as the universal norm instead of another manifestation of the human experience. Refusal to ethnicize the dominant sector tends to privilege the mainstream as the unacknowledged standard of normalcy – but at the cost of masking the socially constructed and ideologically loaded nature of "systemic whiteness." (p. 34)

By avoiding any suggestion that mainstream news media is white-centered, "the universal norm," the status quo persists, and that privileging remains endemic to newsgathering norms. However, mainstream media view themselves as universal, serving *the* public, *all* segments of society, though in reality they tend to underserve non-white communities. Ethnic media center the marginalized voices that are overlooked or under- of misrepresented by the mainstream, but they explicitly recognize the approach. The result is ethnic media still seek out *some* of the institutional voices associated with white supremacy in colonial, patriarchal societies; the voices mainstream newsgathering norms have always privileged. At the same time ethnic media, by the very nature of their mandate, include the voices from their communities left out or under-reported by mainstream journalists. Indigenous television network APTN interviews the First Nations flood evacuees ignored by the other media. A Black-Latino photographer adds authentic context on the true nature of the BLM movement by focusing – not on the limited violence and chaos of some protests – but scenes of compassionate demonstrators consoling a traumatized, conflicted, angry young man. Indigenous journalists covering the Mi'kmaw lobster fishery changed the narrative on mainstream coverage of violent opposition from non-Indigenous lobster fishers by including the voices and fundamental Mi'kmaw perspectives, specifically the fact that the Mi'kmaw right to fish was established by treaty and Supreme Court precedent. These examples demonstrate the value of truly inclusive reporting, whether in mainstream, ethnic, or Indigenous media. They also underscore the importance of having journalists from different backgrounds, with firsthand understanding of these issues, in mainstream newsrooms.

Conclusion

This chapter has combined the scholarship of the past with recent cases from the racial reckoning to better understand the role of white supremacy and systemic racism in newsgathering norms. A colonial history steeped in European superiority has shaped much of the way mainstream news organization have typically framed news coverage. Content has predominantly focused on white values, been produced predominantly by white reporters and editors, for predominantly white audiences. The rhythms and routines have further reinforced white dominance in news coverage by privileging institutional speakers who tend to be male, white, and heterosexual. However, when racialized and Indigenous journalists report, they bring knowledge, lived experience, and empathy resulting in news content that is more authentic, contextual, and often more factual, as demonstrated by examples in this chapters. The lessons for mainstream news seem obvious. Why those lessons have not been taken up more thoroughly is the subject of the next chapter.

References

Alcazaren-Keeley, O. (2020, May 22). *African American media demands comprehensive post-coronavirus reform*. Retrieved from Medium.com: https://medium.com/the-maynard-institute-for-journalism-education/african-american-journalists-are-fighting-for-their-communities-amid-covid-19-872b89d6ecc6.

Anderson, M. C., & Robertson, C. L. (2011). *Seeing red: A history of natives in Canadian newspapers.* Winnipeg: University of Manitoba Press.

Arboine, N. (2020, September 2). *I'm a Black journalist in the UK. That simple fact still makes me unusual.* Retrieved from The Guardian: https://www.theguardian.com/commentisfree/2020/sep/02/black-journalist-uk-media-diversity-white.

Arvanitakis, J., Cage, C., Kaabel, A., Han, C., Hine, A., Hopkins, N., ... Weerakkody, S. U. (2020). *Who gets to tell Australian stories? Putting the spotlight on cultural and linguistic diversity in television news and current affairs.* Retrieved from Media Diversity Australia: https://www.mediadiversityaustralia.org/wp-content/uploads/2020/08/Who-Gets-To-Tell-Australian-Stories_LAUNCH-VERSION.pdf.

Bendixen & Associates. (2005). *The ethnic media in America: The hidden giant in plain sight.* New York: The Center for American Progress, The Leadership Conference on Civil Right Education Fund.

Bialik, K. (2019, February 8). *For the fifth time in a row, the new Congress is the most racially and ethnically diverse ever.* Retrieved November 4, 2020, from Pew Research Center: https://www.pewresearch.org/fact-tank/2019/02/08/for-the-fifth-time-in-a-row-the-new-congress-is-the-most-racially-and-ethnically-diverse-ever/.

Billard, T. J. (2016). Writing in the margins: Mainstream news media representations of transgenderism. *International Journal of Communication, 10,* 4193–4218.

Bishop, S. C. (2016). *U.S. media and migration: Refugee oral histories.* New York: Routledge.

Brown, J. (2020, September 24). *#278 Lobster politics.* Retrieved from Canadaland: https://www.canadaland.com/podcast/278-lobster-politics/.

Campbell, C. P., LeDuff, K. M., & Brown, R. A. (2012). Yes we did? Race, myth and the news revisited. In C. P. Campbell, K. M. LeDuff, C. D. Jenkins, & R. A. Brown, *Race and news: Critical perspectives* (pp. 3–21). New York: Routledge.

Callison, C., & Young, M. L. (2020). *Reckoning: Journalism's limits and possibilities.* New York: Oxford University Press.

Canadian Association of Journalists. (2021, November 25). *Canadian Newsroom Diversity Survey Final Report.* Retrieved from Canadian Association of Journalists: https://caj.ca/images/downloads/diversity_survey_report.pdf.

Canadian Press. (2020, October 30). *Lobster dispute: RCMP release photos of persons of interest in southwest N.S. fish plant arson.* Retrieved from CTV News: https://atlantic.ctvnews.ca/lobster-dispute-rcmp-release-photos-of-persons-of-interest-in-southwest-n-s-fish-plant-arson-1.5167891.

CBC News. (2020, September 18). *Mi'kmaw journalist assesses media coverage of fisheries dispute.* Retrieved from CBC News: https://www.cbc.ca/news/canada/nova-scotia/media-coverage-indigenous-issues-mi-kmaw-fishery-marshall-decision-1.5730472.

Chow-White, P., & McMahon, R. (2011). Examining the "dark past" and "hopeful future" in representations of race and Canada's Truth and Reconcilliation Commission. In I. S. Shaw, J. Lynch, & R. A. Hacket (Eds.), *Expanding peace journalism: Comparative and critical approaches* (pp. 345–373). Sydney: Sydney University Press.

Cisneros, J. D. (2008). Contaminated communities: The metaphor of 'immigrant as pollutant' in media representations of immigration. *Rhetoric and Public Affairs, 11*(4), 569–602.

Clark, B. (2014). Framing Canada's Aboriginal Peoples: A comparative analysis of Indigenous and mainstream television news. *Canadian Journal of Native Studies, 34*(2), 41–64.

De Bruin, J., & Mane, J. (. (2018). Indigenous radio and digital media: Tautoko FM's national and transnational audiences. *Radio Journal: International Studies in Broadcast & Audio Media, 16*(12), 127–140. doi:10.1386/rjao.16.2.127_1.

DeHaas, D., Akutagawa, L., & Spriggs, S. (2019, February 5). *Missing Pieces Report: The 2018 Board Diversity Census of Women and Minorities on Fortune 500 Boards.* Retrieved November 4, 2020, from Harvard Law School Forum on Corporate Governance: https://corpgov.law.harvard.edu/2019/02/05/missing-pieces-report-the-2018-board-diversity-census-of-women-and-minorities-on-fortune-500-boards/.

Deuze, M. (2004). Journalism studies beyond media: On ideology and identity. *Ecquid Novi, 25*(2), 275–293.

Downing, J., & Husband, C. (2005). *Representing 'race': Racisms, ethnicities and media.* London: Sage.

Elian, M. B. (2020, July 29). *In photographing social justice protests, respect means 'looking again'.* Retrieved September 21, 2020, from Nieman Reports: https://niemanreports.org/articles/in-photographing-social-justice-protests-respect-means-looking-again/.

Entman, R. (1993). Framing: Toward clarification of a fractured paradigm. *Journal of Communication, 43*(4), 51–58.

Entman, R. M. (1994). Representation and reality in the portrayal of Blacks on network television news. *Journalism Quarterly, 71*, 9–20.

Entman, R., & Rojecki, A. (2001). *The black image in the white mind: Media and race in America.* Chicago, IL: The University of Chicago Press.

Ericson, R. V., Baranek, P. M., & Chan, J. B. (1989). *Negotiating control: A study of news sources.* Toronto: University of Toronto Press.

Fishman, M. (1980). *Manufacturing the news.* Austin: University of Texas Press.

Fleras, A. (2016). Theorizing minority misrepresentations: Reframing mainstream newsmedia as if white ethnic media. In G. Ruhrmann, Y. Shooman, & P. Widmann, *Media and minorities: Questions on representation from an International perspective* (pp. 21–38). Berlin: Vandenhoeck & Ruprecht.

Gans, H. (1979). *Deciding what's news: A study of CBS Evening News, NBC Nightly News, Newsweek and Time.* New York: Random House.

Georgiou, M. (2005). Diasporic media across Europe: Multicultural societies and the universalism-particularism continuum. *Journal of Ethnic and Migration Studies, 31*(3), 481–498.

Ginsburg, F. (1994). Embedded aesthetics: Creating a discursive space for Indigenous media. *Cultural Anthroplogy, 9*(3), 365–382. Retrieved from http://www.jstor.org/stable/656369.

Gomez-Aguinaga, B. (2021). One Group, Two Worlds? Latino Perceptions of policy salience among mainstream and Spanish-language news consumers. *Social Science Quarterly, 102*(1), 238–258. doi:10.1111/ssqu.12884.

Grenier, É. (2020, June 9). *When it comes to leadership's political parties aren't getting more diverse.* Retrieved November 22, 2020, from CBC: https://www.cbc.ca/news/politics/grenier-leadership-diversity-1.5603626.

Hall, S. (1990). Cultural identity and diaspora. In J. Rutherford, *Identity: Community, culture, difference* (pp. 222–237). London: Lawrence & Wishart.

Hall, S. (1997). The spectacle of the "other". In S. Hall, J. Evans, & S. Nixon, *Representation: Cultural representations and signifying practices* (pp. 225–279). London: Sage Publications.

Harding, R. (2006). Historical representations of aboriginal people in the Canadian news media. *Discourse & Society, 17*(205). doi:10.1177/0957926506058059.

Henry, F., & Tator, C. (2002). *Discourses of domination: Racial bias in the Canadian English-language press.* Toronto: University of Toronto Press.

hooks, b. (2013). *Writing beyond race: Living theory and practice.* London: Routledge.

Jackson, S. J. (2020, June 3). *The headlines that are covering up police violence.* Retrieved October 8, 2020, from The Atlantic: https://www.theatlantic.com/culture/archive/2020/06/george-floyd-protests-what-news-reports-dont-say/612571/.

Jenkins, C. D. (2012). Newsroom diversity and representations of race. In C. P. Campbell, K. M. LeDuff, C. D. Jenkins, & R. A. Brown, *Race and news: Critical perspectives* (pp. 22–42). New York: Routledge.

Johnston, A., & Flamiano, D. (2007). Diversity in mainstream newspapers from the standpoint of journalists of color. *Howard Journal of Communications, 18*, 111–131. doi: 10.1080/10646170701309999.

Jones, S. (2020, June 9). *I'm The Inquirer's only black male news columnist. That speaks to a larger problem.* Retrieved July 7, 2020, from inquirer.com: https://www.inquirer.com/opinion/racism-media-black-reporters-editors-philadelphia-inquirer-pittsburgh-20200609.html.

Knopf, K. (2010). "Sharing our stories with all Canadians": Decolonizing Aboriginal media and Aboriginal media politics in Canada. *American Indian Culture and Research Journal, 34*(1), 89–120.

Lambertus, S. (2004). *Wartime images, peacetime wounds: The media and the Gustafsen Lake standoff.* Toronto: University of Toronto Press.

LeDuff, K. M. (2012). Localizing terror, creating fear in post 9/11 local TV news. In C. P. Campbell, K. M. LeDuff, C. D. Jenkins, & R. A. Brown, *Race and news: Critical perspectives* (pp. 219–231). New York: Routledge.

Leonard, C. (2020, October 23). *Watering down the violence against Mi'kmaw fishermen 'dehumanizes Native people'*. Retrieved from The Discourse: https://thediscourse.ca/okanagan/watering-down-the-violence-against-mikmaw-fishermen-dehumanizes-native-people.

Lopez, M. H. (2013). *What Univision's milestone says about U.S. demographics*. Retrieved from Pew Research Center: https://www.pewresearch.org/fact-tank/2013/07/29/what-univisions-milestone-says-about-u-s-demographics/.

Lopez, O. (2020, June 16). *Trans documentary 'Disclosure' debuts in wake of landmark U.S. LGBT+ ruling*. Retrieved from Reuters: https://www.reuters.com/article/us-usa-lgbt-entertainment-disclosure-trf-idUSKBN23N3K5.

Malik, A., & Fatah, S. (2019, November 11). *Newsrooms not keeping up with changing demographics, study suggests*. Retrieved December 12, 2020, from The Conversation: https://theconversation.com/newsrooms-not-keeping-up-with-changing-demographics-study-suggests-125368.

McCallum, K. (2007). Indigenous violence as a "mediated public crisis". *Communications, Civics, Industry – Australia and New Zealand Communication Association (ANZCA) 2007 Conference Proceedings* (pp. 1–15). Melbourne. Retrieved from http://anzca.net/component/docman/cat_view/17-anzca-07/18-refereed-proceedings.html.

McCue, D. (2021, June 1). *At the desk*. Retrieved from Reporting in Indigenous Communities: https://riic.ca/the-guide/at-the-desk/.

McNair, B. (1998). *The sociology of journalism*. New York: Oxford University Press.

News Leaders Association. (2019, September 10). *2019 Diversity survey: Digital-only platforms drive race and gender inclusion among newsrooms in 2019 ASNE Newsroom Diversity Survey*. Retrieved December 12, 2020, from News Leaders Association: https://www.newsleaders.org/2019-diversity-survey-results.

Nishikawa, K., Towner, T. L., Clawson, R., & Waltenburg, E. (2009). Interviewing the interviewers: Journalistic norms and racial diversity in the newsroom. *The Howard Journal of Communications, 20*, 242–259.

Papper, B. (2020, Setpember 9). *2020 Research: Newsroom diversity*. Retrieved from RTDNA: https://www.rtdna.org/article/2020_research_newsroom_diversity.

Pease, E. C., Smith, E., & Subervi, F. (2001). *The news and race models of excellence project overview: connecting newsroom attitudes toward ethnicity and news content*. St. Petersburg, FL: Poynter Institute for Media Studies.

Rosen, J. (2010, November 10). *The view from nowhere: questions and answers*. Retrieved December 12, 2020, from PressThink: https://pressthink.org/2010/11/the-view-from-nowhere-questions-and-answers/.

Roth, L. (2005). *Something new in the air*. Montreal: McGill-Queen's University Press.

Schudson, M. (1989). The sociology of news production. *Media, Culture & Society, 11*, 263–282. doi:10.1177/016344389011003002

Schudson, M. (2011). *The Sociology of News* (2nd ed.). New York: WW Norton & Company.

Shoemaker, P., & Reese, S. (1996). *Mediating the message: theories of influence on mass media content* (2nd ed.). White Plains, NY: Longman.

Teo, P. (2000). Racism in the news: A critical discourse analysis of news reporting in two Australian Newspapers. *Discourse & Society, 11*(7), 7–49. do i:10.1177/0957926500011001002.

Thomson, T. (2016). Black, white, and a whole lot of gray: How white photojournalists covered race during the 2015 protests at Mizzou. *Visual Communication Quarterly, 23*(4), 223–233. doi:10.1080/15551393.2016.1230473.

Tolley, E. (2016). *Framed: Media coverage of race in Canadian politics.* Vancouver, BC: UBC Press.

Uberoi, E., & Lees, R. (2020, October 23). *Ethnic diversity in politics and public life.* Retrieved from House of Commons Library: https://commonslibrary. parliament.uk/research-briefings/sn01156/.

United States Senate. (2021, January 31). *Ethnic diversity in the senate.* Retrieved from United States Senate: https://www.senate.gov/senators/ EthnicDiversityintheSenate.htm.

van Dijk, T. A. (1991). *Racism and the press.* London: Routledge.

Wallace, L. R. (2019). *The view from somewhere: Undoing the myth of journalistic objectivity.* Chicago, IL: The University of Chicago Press.

Weston, M. A. (1996). *Native Americans in the news: Images of Indians in the twentieth century press.* Westport, CT: Greenwood Press.

Wilkes, R., Corrigall-Brown, C., & Ricard, D. (2010). Nationalism and media coverage of indigenous people's collective action in Canada. *American Indian Culture and Research Journal, 34*(4), 41–59.

Wilson, C. C., & Gutierrez, F. (1995). *Race, multiculturalism, and the media.* Thousand Oaks, CA: Sage Publications.

Wilson, C. C., Gutierrez, F., & Chao, L. (2013). *Racism, sexism, and the media: Multicultural issues into the new communications age* (4th ed.). Thousand Oaks, CA: Sage.

Women in Journalism. (2020, September 16). *A week in British newsrooms.* Retrieved from Women in Journalism: https://womeninjournalism.co.uk/ lack-diversity-british-newsrooms/.

Yu, S. S. (2019). Ethnic media and accessibility: Online English-language ethnic media in the U.S. In S. S. Yu, *Ethnic media in the digital age* (pp. 66–78). New York: Routledge.

4   Five Decades of Diversity Measures

Introduction

In 1968, the Kerner Commission in the United States called for the hiring of Black reporters to address the one-sided news coverage of urban unrest at the height of the civil rights movement, and to provide a much needed context for the racism and segregation faced by people of color. In Canada, The Royal Commission on Aboriginal Peoples (RCAP) made similar recommendations for news media in 1996. News organizations in the United Kingdom were challenged to embrace diversity in the wake of the racial murder of Stephen Lawrence, a young Black man, in 1993. Australia grappled with a racist immigration policy through the 1970s, high death rates in custody of Indigenous Peoples, and calls for Indigenous participation in media production through the Eighties and Nineties. In fact, in most Western societies calls for diversity and inclusion by racialized and Indigenous Peoples prompted news organizations, professional associations, and journalism schools to initiate recruiting, mentorship, and scholarship initiatives aimed at boosting newsroom participation for non-white staff. This chapter looks at those measures and reflects on a body of research that identifies why the results failed to meet expectations, tying it to the experiences of racialized and Indigenous journalists referenced in Chapter 2. Journalists of color often find there are too few like them in the newsroom, and fewer still in the executive suites. They are expected to fulfill the role of sensitivity readers on copy related to race, but when they raise concerns, they meet resistance from management. There is also a "burden of representation" in which they are expected to cover their own communities but in a way that is consistent with the expectations of their largely white assignment editors. As one Indigenous journalist observes, their reporting on their own race and culture is frequently questioned, but at the same time, it can be all they

DOI: 10.4324/9781003261544-5

are allowed to cover. In the end, the news media's attempts at diversity and inclusion too often fail to take into account the very perspectives they claim to want.

Early Efforts: Multicultural Awareness and Hiring

Grainy archival footage on the CBC's website from 1970 shows a panel of ten white men and one white woman sitting on a news set in the familiar semi-circle, a news desk in the middle, ashtrays distributed among the participants. A new federal policy decision on Canadian content in domestic radio and television had pre-empted the usual evening fare, *The Nature of Things*, a decision that is hard to imagine 50 years later. However, what is truly striking about the footage today is the obvious lack of diversity: only one woman on an 11-person panel, no Indigenous people, no people of color. By all accounts, news media across the Western world were similarly white, resulting in a news discourse that was Eurocentric and homogenous, justifying military incursions in developing colonial nations, the exclusionary policies of the cold war, and racist immigration systems. Racialized and Indigenous Peoples were slow to be embraced by the white mainstream news media of the day and their audiences, as either journalists or news sources. The first Black woman to report on television in the United Kingdom, Barbara Blake Hannah, made her debut on the evening news on Thames TV in 1968, but was inexplicably fired nine months later (PressFrom, 2019). Her skill as a journalist was obvious, but "she was never well received by her colleagues or the predominantly white audience" and her producer admitted to her that the station was "under pressure from viewers who called in daily to say: 'Get that n***** off our screens'." It was only a few years earlier, in 1962, that Malvin R. Goode became the first Black network TV reporter in the United States at ABC, apparently "after baseball icon Jackie Robinson complained to the network executives that there weren't enough Black reporters on air" (Associated Press, 2020).

The civil rights movement was gaining momentum in the United States through the 1960s, and it was not too long before Robinson's observations would be further validated in the form of a major government report. The Kerner Commission, referenced in Chapter 2, condemned the American press for – "along with the country as a whole" – basking in "a white world... with white men's eyes" (National Advisory Commission on Civil Disorders, 1968, p. 213). It cited instances of inaccurate, sensational, and even fabricated coverage of rioting and violence in Black neighborhoods (p. 202). The commission determined that news media had contributed to a "black-white schism" in American society: "If what the white American reads in the newspapers or sees on television conditions his expectation of what is ordinary and normal in the larger society, he will neither understand nor accept the black American" (p. 211). Recommendations included calling on editors to review their own content and its potential impact on Black audiences, developing Black news sources, contacts and beats, looking to the Black press for guidance on the range of stories to tell, and hiring Black reporters as well as "editors, writers and commentators," noting that "tokenism... is no longer enough" (p. 211). The report concluded "if the media are to report with understanding, wisdom and sympathy on the problems of the cities and the problems of the black man... they must employ, promote and listen to Negro journalists" (p. 212).

The report set in motion diversity initiatives in news media and professional associations, but before long the "the heady advances of the civil rights era of the 1960s had stalled" (Delgado & Stefancic, 2017, p. 4). When progress toward more equitable newsrooms started to wane, the American Society of News Editors (ASNE), now known as the News Leaders Association, stepped up with its first "Minorities Committee" in 1977, and a year later came up with five recommendations:

1 The commitment to recruit, train and hire minorities needs urgently to be rekindled. This is simply the right thing to do. It is also in the newspaper industry's economic self-interest.
2 There should be at least an annual accounting by ASNE of minority employment, including not just total jobs but types of positions held.
3 There should be special emphasis on increasing the number of minority newsroom executives.
4 Small papers should especially be encouraged to add minority members to their staffs.
5 Leaders among minority journalists have urge the industry to set a goal of minority employment by the year 2000 equivalent to the percentage of minority persons within the national population. The committee believes this is a fair and attainable goal (News Leaders Association, 2021).

These policies not only reflected the Kerner commission's report but advanced the mandate with an annual newsroom census starting in 1978 to determine the level of participation by racialized news staff and establishing a demographic benchmark based on the non-white percentage of the US population. The Radio-Television Digital News

Association (RTDNA) would launch a similar, biennial "census" in broadcast media 17 years later (Papper, 2020), another tool to measure the actual progress of hiring initiatives in US media. Outside the United States, however, such metrics were generally deployed only more recently and often inconsistently, such as individual studies (see Miller, 2005; Spears, Seydegart, & Zulinov, 2010). While policies and legislation in Canada, the United Kingdom, and Australia were introduced to support wider goals of women's rights, multiculturalism, and anti-racism, diverse hiring practices in newsrooms lagged behind.

As with Black Lives Matter in 2020, civil rights action in the United States spurred racialized communities in other parts of the world to fight discrimination and pressure their governments to take action. The United Kingdom, Canada, and Australia all had explicitly racist immigration policies in the 20th century, the latter's part of the "White Australia Policy" which also relied on forced deportation of Asians and Pacific Islanders (National Museum Australia, 2021). Mass immigration after World War II brought a huge influx of non-British migrants to Australia, giving rise to foreign language newspapers and radio programming. For some Australians hearing languages other than English on the airwaves was seen as "subversive" and the Australian Broadcasting Control Board (ABCB) limited such content to 2.5 per cent of airtime on commercial radio (Ang, Hawkins, & Dabboussy, 2008, p. 15). By 1973 the government of the day removed all racial component of immigration policy and would begin to establish policies of multiculturalism, though Australian media at the time remained "relentlessly white" (p. 8). Indigenous Peoples in Australia were also engaged in an ongoing struggle over territorial rights and segregation, though virtually invisible in news media, except for coverage related to crime and social issues. Even after the Mabo case in 1992 recognized Indigenous rights to colonized land, and the disturbing findings of the Deaths in Custody inquiry, Indigenous voices remained tremendously under-represented (Downing & Husband, 2005, p. 119). Through the late Seventies and early Eighties, "the demand for more Aboriginal participation and visibility in the Australian mediascape" steadily increased "not only for local access to video in remote areas, but also for more Aboriginal representation on mainstream national television" (Ginsburg, 1994, p. 369). This was addressed in part with the creation of the Special Broadcasting Service (SBS), a public broadcaster, offering multicultural radio and then television programming in the late 1970s (Ang, Hawkins, & Dabboussy, 2008).

Around the time of that cigarette-smoking, exclusively white and almost entirely male panel of pundits and journalists was discussing broadcast policy on the CBC set, described earlier in this chapter, Canada was just months away from becoming the first nation in the world to adopt an official policy of multiculturalism. While this measure burnished Canada's reputation as a progressive and tolerant country – an image many would argue is exaggerated – it was also politically expedient for the Liberal government of the day. At the time, nationalism was rising in Quebec, Indigenous Peoples were demanding civil rights, and "third-force" immigrant groups, mostly of Eastern European descent, were calling for greater recognition (McRoberts, 1997, p. 122). In spite of the newfound mandate for multiculturalism, the government's priority for newspapers was not the nature of the content or its impact on marginalized segments of society, but rather the concentration of ownership in the industry, the subject of the *Davey Report* in 1970. The first Canadian studies of race, ethnicity, and media were published in the 1970s, supporting the criticisms of minority communities that news depictions featured "unrelenting negativity in their portrayal" of those groups (Mahtani, 2001, p. 103). In concert with developing multicultural policy at the federal level, the findings of these studies were eventually reflected in the work of the Special Committee on Participation of Visible Minorities in Canadian Society, in a report titled "Equality Now!". It lauds some of the early efforts of the CBC to "train a variety of visible minority persons" – only eight positions – and made 15 recommendations including setting "standards for reporting on visible minorities" and "encouraging the hiring and training of visible minorities within all areas of the media" (Special Committee on the Participation of Visible Minorities in Canadian Society, 1984, pp. 100–102). In making the recommendations the committee observed that the media "have not only been slow in initiating change but in many areas have lagged behind the Canadian people in positive attitude changes towards visible minorities" (p. 95). Another federal government body would eventually articulate similar concerns with regard to the Indigenous experience with the release of the Report of the Royal Commission on Aboriginal Peoples, the product of 178 days of hearings. It found there was a "need for accurate information and realistic portrayals of Aboriginal people," pointing out the persistent stereotypes whereby "Many Canadians know Aboriginal people only as noble environmentalists, angry warriors or pitiful victims. A full picture of their humanity is simply not available in the media" (Royal Commission on Aboriginal Peoples, 1996).

Ottawa sought to address such issues with the Employment Equity Act (1986), which is still in effect, requiring employers from federally regulated industries, government institutions, and crown corporations to ensure barriers to employment are removed for people in four groups: Women, Indigenous Peoples, people with disabilities, and "visible minorities" (Canadian Human Rights Commission, 2009). Employers covered by the Act are also required to maintain records on hiring practices, and file annual reports. Since the broadcast industry is federally regulated, television and radio news operations are included in this legislation; newspapers and magazines are not. Broadcasters are required to file diversity reports to the Canadian Radio-television Telecommunication Commission (CRTC) on their compliance with the Act. However, Murray (2009) argues these submissions typically do not address specific measures to improve news coverage, such as "efforts to diversify news sources, stories, and on-air personalities" (p. 695). A recent report submitted by Corus Entertainment, which owns Global News, shows companies answer specific questions about the diversity of news staff and sources, but offer few metrics (Corus Entertainment, 2019). For example, the report states "Indigenous peoples, immigrants from a variety of ethnic backgrounds, persons with disabilities, people of varying sexual orientations, and people with differing religious and economic backgrounds are all newsmakers as well as experts that contribute to Corus' news programming" (p. 18), but does not mention whether there was an increase or decrease in those sources from the previous year, or how representative its use of sources is compared to demographic benchmarks. The Corus report details semi-annual "meet and greet" events with "local diverse communities" (p. 22), as well as donations for Indigenous scholarships and internship plans but fails to mention the hiring of any Indigenous reporters, producers, or hosts.

Regardless of the country or continent, diversity programs have followed a familiar prescription of measures around the world. They typically include boosting awareness with multicultural and anti-racism training, recruiting "culturally diverse applicants," and "training and mentoring schemes" offered by unions, individual news organizations, and professional associations (Siapera, 2010, pp. 88–89). These measures can create an appearance of diversity activity, though in practice – as with the CRTC's diversity reporting policy in Canada – the impact is negligible. All too often diversity initiatives become "a rehearsal of collective ethical virtue," but given the importance of more accurate and equitable reporting, "may generate a dangerous illusion of substantive change" (Downing & Husband, 2005, p. 163). In the United Kingdom, "race awareness training" was pursued through the 1970s and 1980s, but "was substantially irrelevant to changing corporate equal opportunities practices" (Sivanandan, 1981; Gurnah, 1989; cited in Downing & Husband, 2005).

This seems to be the case in Canada as well, where not only are most reporters and editors, white, but there are "very few programs for increasing staff diversity and most outlets express very little concern for doing so" (Tolley, 2016, p. 179). A pair of industry initiatives offer examples of the approach generally taken in Canada and other Western nations. The Canadian Association of Broadcasters (CAB) convened a task force on diversity, and its report included a section of "best practices" for news organizations based on steps taken in other countries. The CAB called for four broad sets of measures: recruiting and hiring of non-white reporters, policies designed to prevent the "pigeonholing" of racialized journalists into coverage of their own communities, building banks of non-white sources and experts (the so-called "rainbow rolodex"), and cultural awareness/community outreach programs (Canadian Association of Broadcasters, 2004, pp. 36–42). The Canadian arm of the Radio-Television News Directors Association (RTNDA Canada) also published a guide for its members, *Everyone's Story: Reflecting Canada's Diversity* (RTNDA Canada, 2006). It too emphasized hiring racialized and Indigenous news staff, but also discussed stereotypes and "diversifying" news coverage (RTNDA Canada, 2006, p. 36). The guide features glossaries, direction on preferred usage, and capitalization for a variety of marginalized groups, and "diversity checklists," calling on editorial staff to routinely reflect on their coverage to assess "the cumulative impact of our coverage" (p.15). Aside from concerns over the issue of "pigeon-holing" there is no exploration of how best to deploy non-white workers, how they might be supported, or details on ways to ensure equitable compensation and promotion for marginalized staff.

As the next section demonstrates, those missing elements were critical. After decades of hiring and awareness programs, journalists of color are still under-represented, and the news media remain predominantly white. The racial reckoning of 2020 offers further confirmation of the inability of news organizations to change the script. Hiring and multicultural awareness alone do not work.

The "Mysterious Alchemy" of Diversity

The most recent data on journalists of color, and racialized and Indigenous news staff in the field of journalism show participation rates well below "parity," the demographic benchmark or proportion of those groups in broader society. The ASNE initial employment survey in 1978 came with a goal of achieving parity by 2000. When the new millennium arrived and the target was missed, the organization aimed for proportional participation by 2025. The most recent survey shows there is still work to do to meet the deadline, finding that "people of color made up 21.9 per cent of the salaried workforce," including 7.5 per cent Black and three per cent Asian news staff (News Leaders Association, 2019). The U.S. census from the same year shows people of color account for about 39 per cent of the American population; Blacks and Asians make up 13.4 and 5.9 per cent respectively (United States Census Bureau, 2019). The survey also found that newsroom managers are overwhelmingly white at just over 81 per cent. In Canada, newsroom demographic data have been scarce, but in late 2021 the Canadian Association of Journalists (CAJ) released the most comprehensive survey to date. Data were collected from 209 newsroom and 3,873 journalists. Close to 75 per cent of all news staff were white, compared to about 73 per cent in Canadian society, 6.4 per cent were Indigenous versus 4.9 per cent in the national population, and 18.6 per cent identified as visible minority, a category that represents 22.3 per cent of Canadians (Canadian Association of Journalists, 2021, p. 7). However, while the overall numbers appear to approach parity in the overall population, the report's authors suggested this was misleading. They noted that Indigenous and racialized staff tended "be concentrated in a handful of large newsrooms," notably the CBC and APTN (p. 5). They pointed out that "about eight in ten newsrooms have no Black or Indigenous journalists" (p. 6), 84 per cent "employ no Indigenous journalists," and "almost half exclusively employ white journalists" (p. 5). The survey found 81.9 per cent of newsroom supervisors are white (p. 7). Outside the CAJ's research, an analysis of columnists at Canada's three largest newspapers found that 89 per cent are white (Malik & Fatah, 2019).

In the United Kingdom, a study by the National Council for the Training of Journalists found "that around 94% of journalists are white, despite BAME [Black, Asian, and minority ethnic] people making up 14% of the population" (Batchelor-Hunt & Walawakar, 2020). Chapter 1 featured a study of British news outlets by Women in Journalism that documented a profound lack of racialized journalists in both print and broadcast. In the study's sample period "not a single black reporter was featured on the front page of any of the newspapers" and "only 12% of [television] reporters [were] from a Black or BAME background" (Women in Journalism, 2020). In radio, the analysis showed "out of a total of 723 prime-time radio reporter appearances... just four were by black women." A recent report by Media Diversity Australia and a group of academics looking at TV networks revealed "a staggering 75 per cent of on-air talent on news and current affairs programs are from Anglo-Celtic backgrounds" (Gillespie, 2020). The analysis showed Channel Nine had "just 2.9% of on-air talent from non-European backgrounds," while Channel 7 was slightly more diverse at 4.8 per cent. Among Australia's public broadcasters, "9.1 per cent of ABC's on-air news talent was non-European and 5 percent Indigenous, compared to SBS which had 76.6 percent of on-air news talent coming from non-European backgrounds and 0.2 percent Indigenous." The participation rates for non-white journalists at senior levels is even worse. A Reuters Institute examination of news outlets in Germany, Brazil, South Africa, the United Kingdom and the United States showed 15 per cent of top editors are "non-white, despite the fact that, on average, 42 per cent of the general population across all five countries are non-white;" and when South Africa is taken out of the sample, "5 per cent of the top editors are non-white, compared to, on average, 30 per cent of the general population" (Robertson, Selva, & Nielsen, 2021).

When racialized and Indigenous journalists spoke out through the racial reckoning of 2020, they made it quite clear why diversity measures have failed. Systemic racism was never just an issue for news organizations to capture in their reporting, it has always been a negative force in their own newsrooms as well. In theory, the expectation was that non-white journalists would bring their lived experience, perspectives, and community connections to the news discourse, addressing issues of under- and misrepresentation, adding much needed context and equity. Undoubtedly that is the case with much of the reporting by Indigenous and racialized journalists (Tolley, 2016, p. 181). Wilson, Gutierrez, and Chao (2013), suggest that "increased employment of non-whites" in news staff should help to establish "a functional information surveillance system that promotes social understanding and alleviates unwarranted fears based on racial, cultural or gender prejudices" (p. 205). However, newsrooms too often did little to address the dominant white bias that pervades news operations, besides add a few faces of color to the mix, prompting a skepticism captured by one journalist's comments in a diversity study, who observed that "by some mysterious alchemy, the whole task of providing better coverage of minority issues seems to have become tied to the effort to bring more minority individuals into the newsroom" (Pritchard & Stonbely, 2007, p. 233).

As we saw in the data from Chapter 2, as well as the research covered in Chapter 3, the white supremacy that has run through newsgathering norms and journalism's ethical canon shapes the news discourse profoundly, even when Indigenous and racialized journalists are present to offer some "surveillance." Journalist Isaac Bailey made the point succinctly during the racial reckoning, writing "No one in the United States is immune to the influence of white supremacy, not even a black Southerner like me" (Bailey, 2020). An early study on the impact of diverse staff looked specifically at television news in Chicago found that Black anchors "spoke from the same perspective as white anchors; there was no difference between their reporting, which of course is what their job descriptions demanded" (Entman, 1992, p. 357). Quantitative studies support this assertion as well. An examination of 723 national television news stories in Canada found that racialized journalists incorporated non-white sources into their reporting at a slightly higher rate than their white colleagues, but still over-represented white sources (Clark, 2013). Racialized reporters included non-white speakers in close to 15 per cent of source-appearances, compared to nine per cent by White journalists (p. 37). The assumption has always been that non-white news staff would counter the over-reliance on white voices. Researchers in the United States conducted similar investigations of source use by white and non-white TV journalists during election campaigns (Zeldes & Fico, 2005; Zeldes, Fico, & Didi, 2007). They too found all reporters, regardless of gender and ethnicity are much more likely to feature white, male sources, although female and racialized reporters incorporate diverse sources at a higher rate than white reporters (Zeldes & Fico, 2005, pp. 379–382).

The mysterious alchemy simply is not enough to counter the white dominance that runs through news values, ethics, and newsgathering norms. A study of BBC local television news reveals non-white producers must deal with "the burden of representation" whereby they are "wary of becoming too closely involved with a particular community and its representatives since this could be interpreted as compromising their claim to professionalism" (Cottle, 2000, pp. 106, 112). The "corporate context" of the BBC forces those racialized news staff to be professionally detached, distancing them "from those communities and groups who could otherwise serve to keep them in touch with, and to some extent accountable to, community interests" (p. 106). However, the study also found those same journalists were willing to take action when they recognized "the need to counter dominant images" about their community (p. 112). A US study of Black and Latino journalists also exposed how professional pressure to be objective, "to 'act' like journalists, not like minorities" can constrain the reporter's ability to authentically report on racialized groups, though interviewees felt the need to "represent," to "wave the red flag" or ask "the pointed question" over inequitable or stereotypic editorial decisions as well (Nishikawa et al., 2009, p. 255).

The racial reckoning in journalism offered extensive, detailed evidence supporting the earlier scholarship discussed above. Indigenous and racialized journalists described their encounters with white editors who scolded them "it's not about race," or accused them of "having an agenda," or sanitized their copy by removing direct, accurate language lest it come off as biased in the view of (white) audiences. They sought to fulfill the role of surveillance system and "wave the red flag" over stereotypic news coverage of Black Lives Matter protests, stories that included no Black sources but played up conflict and fear. In some cases, they were disciplined for their efforts. One journalist, a Black woman, explained the position racialized news staff so often find themselves in: "There seems to be the assumption that we cannot coexist with the journalistic standards of being fair and balanced and impartial. Really, what we are fighting for, what we've always been fighting for, is just the truth" (Mattar, 2020). While journalists of color took their places – typically with few racialized mentors or colleagues – in mainstream newsroom, they also advocated for greater diversity. Gustavo Arellano, writing in the *Los Angeles Times'* special issue on race, told the story of decades worth of efforts on the part of Latino staff "to seed Latinos and Latino coverage through all parts of the paper" (Arellano, 2020). "But again and again, the efforts sputtered because editors couldn't get their minds around planning for a mañana in Southern California when Latinos would dominate the civic and cultural life of the region. Mañana is now."

Persistent Issues of Retention

In 2018, Canadian journalist Sunny Dhillon wrote a first-person article for Medium titled, "Journalism While Brown and When to Walk Away." It is the story of how he finally cleaned out his desk at *The Globe and Mail's* Vancouver bureau one day, weighing "letting other people of color down" against staying at the publication when "each instance in which your outlet drops the ball on a matter of race can feel like a body blow" (Dhillon, 2018). His last story assignment had been to cover the municipal election in Vancouver in which all ten councilors elected were white in a city where "45 per cent of the people are of Asian descent." However, he was told by his bureau chief to focus more on the fact that eight women had been voted in, and less on the racial make-up, after he had conducted several interviews with unsuccessful candidates of color. When he expressed his disagreement with that editorial direction, he was told the newspaper was not a "democracy."

> I decided to leave *The Globe and Mail* because that final conversation inside the bureau chief's office crystallized what I had felt: What I brought to the newsroom did not matter. And it was at that moment that being a person of color at a paper and in an industry that does not have enough of us — particularly at the top — felt more futile than ever before.

Dhillon's frustration boiled over in part because the solutions to the problem of diversity in Canadian newsrooms seemed so obvious: "hire more people of color, hear their voices, elevate them to positions of power or prominence" (Dhillon, 2018). Of course, Dhillon had been hired; his problem, experienced by Indigenous and racialized journalists in other Western countries, was not being heard and not being able to work with other, non-white supervisors and managers.

Getting diverse staff into newsrooms has proved to be less of a challenge than keeping them there. As the findings in Chapter 2 so clearly demonstrate, the workplace is fraught for staff who are racialized or Indigenous: their journalism is challenged as biased, they are expected to lead diversity initiatives, they encounter constant microaggressions, they deal with inequitable pay and promotion structures, and as a result of all of these, they experience higher degrees of stress. While they navigate these challenges in the work environment itself, they also see an industry that too frequently fails to report fairly and truthfully on marginalized groups, and questions their role in it, just as Sunny Dhillon described. In his *New York Times* op-ed, Wesley Lowery mentioned this too: "While these two battles may seem superficially separate, in reality, the failure of the mainstream press to accurately cover black communities is intrinsically linked with its failure to employ, retain and listen to black people" (Lowery, 2020). This is not a new phenomenon, but an ongoing reflection of the white supremacy that continues to influence the norms of practice and ethical ideology.

Diversity measures over the decades have "felt cyclical" to journalists of color (Miller, 2020). Affirmative action "sparked" some initiatives, but the proportion of non-white reporters in the United States actually fell between 2007 and 2015 to levels not seen since 1989. Newspapers were especially hard hit by the technological disruption of the internet so that "the attempt to reach the goal of having more diverse newsrooms has been hindered by an industry-wide problem to keep newspapers profitable and running" (Jenkins, 2012, p. 39). At the same time, it was pointed out that the industry should not neglect "one problem to fix the other," a view expressed by Charlotte Hall, a former ASNE president, who said "the loss of journalists is a loss of democracy ... the loss of people of color for our newsrooms is especially disturbing because our future depends on our ability to serve multicultural audiences" (p. 39). Nonetheless, there are analyses that found "most newsrooms have 'defensive' cultures and are 'resistant to change'" (p. 34). While some white editors recognized the value of a diverse newsroom others did not, as was the case with this manager of a Midwest daily, commenting in an ASNE survey that "generally, hiring minorities means reducing standards temporarily. Except for one reporter and one news editor, every minority person we've hired in 10 years was less qualified than a concurrently available white" (Wilson, Gutierrez, & Chao, 2013, p. 226). Given such attitudes, it is clear why Pease and Smith (1991) found almost three-quarters of racialized journalists said their publications provided substandard coverage of racial issues, two-thirds felt race played a role in story assignment and promotions, and over 70 per cent said editors questioned their reporting abilities (p. 40). They concluded that "journalists of color feel themselves besieged by their race" (p. 23).

Multicultural training and greater awareness of colonial, racist, and exclusionary history undoubtedly provides deeper context for white reporters covering issues of race. However, if the newsroom is not receptive to listening and learning about the racial experience, the scholarship shows everything from hiring to rainbow rolodexes will have limited impact in the quest for more equitable news coverage. Through the racial reckoning in 2020 there were dozens of examples from Indigenous and racialized news workers describing instances where they were shut down when they confronted their news organizations for falling back on familiar patterns of sensationalism, fear mongering, and stereotypes. At Global News in Canada, two former staff members said "they were tone-policed when they raised concerns about the workplace" (Krishnan, 2020). One sent an email to the company's diversity consultant, DiversiPro, stating "they had been 'called into a meeting with HR to discuss the ways in which I am racist to white men' and was told, 'My comments about Canadian media's ongoing whiteness problem make some white men around me uncomfortable.'"

Despite that ongoing whiteness problem, and its impact on retention rates for diverse news staff, just about everyone agrees that hiring – diversifying newsrooms – is still the key to a new era of inclusive coverage. What seems to be increasingly recognized now is that recruiting needs to go beyond tokenism, it needs to be sustained, and it needs to target all skill levels, from the entry level reporters and production assistants to managing editors and news directors. When racialized and Indigenous reporters are the "lone voice" in their newsrooms, they "might well be drowned out by a chorus of often more senior and influential white voices" (Nishikawa et al., 2009, p. 255). What is needed is *"larger* numbers of racially diverse journalists" to counter the white-dominant dynamic (emphasis added, Jenkins, 2012, p. 35) to the point where non-white news staff comprise "a critical mass" to ensure newsrooms "make real changes in news outputs... whether minority journalists have a positive impact on news coverage may depend on how many journalists are present who share that goal" (Nishikawa et al., 2009, p. 255). As "alchemy" for more equitable reporting, hiring will only work if the manifold issues undermining retention are addressed.

Conclusion

After more than 50 years of efforts to diversify newsrooms and bring about a more authentic, equitable style of reporting, the news workforce remains predominantly white in Western nations. The work environment for racialized and Indigenous journalists is fraught. Past scholarship describes the challenges for non-white reporters, starting with the expectations to act as bulwarks against stereotypic and sensational content. It is a role white journalists are not asked to fulfill in the same way. When journalists of color do flag issues with news coverage they are frequently met with resistance, or questions about their professionalism. The racial reckoning overwhelmingly confirmed this dynamic, as well as the frustration and weariness of racialized news workers. This results in poor retention and an endless loop of hiring initiatives that never manage to fill required deficits in diverse staff. The question the industry needs to ask is how do you break the cycle? The next chapter examines the responses by news organizations to the calls for change from Indigenous and racialized workers through the racial reckoning, highlighting the successes as well as the missed opportunities.

References

Ang, I., Hawkins, G., & Dabboussy, L. (2008). *The SBS story.* Sydney: UNSW Press.

Arellano, G. (2020, September 27). *Column: for Latinos and the L.A. Times, a complicated past—and a promising future.* Retrieved from Los Angeles Times: https://www.latimes.com/opinion/story/2020-09-27/los-angeles-times-historical-latino-coverage.

Associated Press. (2020, December 14). *Little known black history fact: the first Black network news reporter.* Retrieved from BlackAmericaWeb: https://www.google.com/search?q=first+black+TV+reporter+US&rlz= 1C1JZAP_enCA894CA894&oq=first+black+TV+reporter+US&aqs= chrome..69i57j0i22i3012j0i39012j69i6413.11746j0j15&sourceid=chrome& ie=UTF-8.

Bailey, I. (2020, May 29). *George Floyd, Ahmaud Arbery, and one journalist's painfully honest self-examination on racism.* Retrieved August 8, 2020, from Nieman Reports: https://niemanreports.org/articles/george-floyd-ahmaud-arbery-and-one-journalists-painfully-honest-self-examination-on-racism/.

Batchelor-Hunt, N., & Walawakar, A. (2020, September 2). *'I could speak more freely': The enduring need for Black British media.* Retrieved from Each Other: https://eachother.org.uk/i-could-speak-more-freely-the-enduring-need-for-black-british-media/.

Canadian Association of Broadcasters. (2004, July). *Reflecting Canadians: best practices for cultural diversity in Private Television. A report by the Task Force for Cultural Diversity on Television.* Retrieved September 9, 2010, from cab-acr.ca: http://www.cab-acr.ca/english/social/diversity/taskforce/ report/cdtf_report_jul04.pdf.

Canadian Association of Journalists. (2021, November 25). *Canadian newsroom diversity survey final report.* Retrieved from Canadian Association of Journalists: https://caj.ca/images/downloads/diversity_survey_report.pdf.

Canadian Human Rights Commission. (2009, August 27). *Frequently asked questions about employment equity.* Retrieved October 3, 2010, from Canadian Human Right Commission: http://www.chrc-ccdp.ca/publications/ ee_faq_ee-en.asp.

Clark, B. (2013). Reflecting which Canada? A source analysis of Canadian network television news. *International Journal of Diverse Identities, 12*(1), 33–45.

Corus Entertainment. (2019). *Annual/monthly reports filed by broadcasting industry players.* Retrieved from Canadian Radio-television and Telecommunications Commission: https://crtc.gc.ca/eng/BCASTING/ann_rep/annualrp.htm#shawmedia.

Cottle, S. (2000). A rock and a hard place: Making ethnic minority television. In S. Cottle (Ed.), *Ethnic minorities and the media* (pp. 100–117). Buckingham, United Kingdom: Open University Press.

Delgado, R., & Stefancic, J. (2017). *Critical race theory: an introduction* (3rd ed.). New York: New York University Press.

Dhillon, S. (2018, October 29). *Journalism while Brown and when to walk away.* Retrieved from Medium: https://level.medium.com/journalism-while-brown-and-when-to-walk-away-9333ef61de9a.

Downing, J., & Husband, C. (2005). *Representing 'race': Racisms, ethnicities and media.* London: Sage.

Entman, R. M. (1992). Blacks in the news: Television, modern racism and cultural change. *Journalism Quarterly, 69*(2), 341–361.

Gillespie, E. (2020, August 17). *Karl Stefanovic under fire after comments on media diversity report.* Retrieved from SBS News: https://www.sbs.com.au/news/the-feed/karl-stefanovic-under-fire-after-comments-on-media-diversity-report.

Ginsburg, F. (1994). Embedded aesthetics: Creating a discursive space for Indigenous media. *Cultural Anthroplogy, 9*(3), 365–382. Retrieved from http://www.jstor.org/stable/656369.

Jenkins, C. D. (2012). Newsroom diversity and representations of race. In C. P. Campbell, K. M. LeDuff, C. D. Jenkins, & R. A. Brown, *Race and news: Critical perspectives* (pp. 22–42). New York: Routledge.

Krishnan, M. (2020, August 20). *In the midst of a race reckoning, Global News laid off some of its most vocal internal critics.* Retrieved September 2, 2020, from Vice News: https://www.vice.com/en/article/jgx4ek/in-the-midst-of-a-race-reckoning-global-news-laid-off-some-of-its-most-vocal-internal-critics.

Lowery, W. (2020, June 23). *A reckoning over objectivity, led by Black journalists.* Retrieved July 7, 2020, from The New York Times: https://www.nytimes.com/2020/06/23/opinion/objectivity-black-journalists-coronavirus.html.

Mahtani, M. (2001). Representing minorities: Canadian media and minority identities. *Canadian Ethnic Studies, 33*(3), 99–133.

Malik, A., & Fatah, S. (2019, November 11). *Newsrooms not keeping up with changing demographics, study suggests.* Retrieved December 12, 2020, from The Conversation: https://theconversation.com/newsrooms-not-keeping-up-with-changing-demographics-study-suggests-125368

Mattar, P. (2020, August 21). *Objectivity is a privilege afforded to white journalists.* Retrieved September 1, 2020, from The Walrus: https://thewalrus.ca/objectivity-is-a-privilege-afforded-to-white-journalists/.

McRoberts, K. (1997). *Misconceiving Canada: The struggle for national unity.* Toronto: Oxford University Press.

Miller, E. (2020, September 1). *How two local newsrooms are sewing diversity into the fabric of their organizations.* Retrieved from Poynter.: https://www.poynter.org/business-work/2020/how-two-local-newsrooms-are-sewing-diversity-into-the-fabric-of-their-organizations/.

Miller, J. (2005). Who's telling the news? Racial representation among news gatherers in Canada's daily newsrooms. *International Journal of Diversity in Organizations, Communities and Nations, 5*, 1–10.

Murray, C. A. (2009). Designing monitoring to promote cultural diversification in TV. *Canadian Journal of Communication, 34*(4), 675–699.

National Advisory Commission on Civil Disorders. (1968). *The Report of the National Advisory Commission on Civil Disorders.* New York: New York Times Publications.

National Museum Australia. (2021, August 14). *Defining moments: end of the White Australia policy.* Retrieved from National Museum Australia: https://www.nma.gov.au/defining-moments/resources/end-of-white-australia-policy.

News Leaders Association. (2019, September 10). *2019 Diversity survey: Digital-only platforms drive race and gender inclusion among newsrooms in 2019 ASNE Newsroom Diversity Survey.* Retrieved December 12, 2020, from News Leaders Association: https://www.newsleaders. org/2019-diversity-survey-results

News Leaders Association. (2021, August 14). *ASNE diversity history.* Retrieved from News Leaders Association: https://members.newsleaders.org/ content.asp?pl=28&sl=15&contentid=57.

Nishikawa, K., Towner, T. L., Clawson, R., & Waltenburg, E. (2009). Interviewing the interviewers: journalistic norms and racial diversity in the newsroom. *The Howard Journal of Communications, 20,* 242–259.

Papper, B. (2020, September 9). *2020 Research: newsroom diversity.* Retrieved from RTDNA: https://www.rtdna.org/article/2020_research_newsroom_ diversity.

Pease, T., & Smith, J. F. (1991). The newsroom barometer: Job satisfaction and the impact of racial diversity at US daily newspapers. *Ohio Journalism Monographs, 1.*

PressFrom. (2019, October 31). *'I was treated with disgust': The first black female journalist on UK TV.* Retrieved from Press, from: https://pressfrom. info/uk/news/world/us-news/-368504-i-was-treated-with-disgust-the-firstblack-female-journalist-on-uk-tv.html.

Pritchard, D., & Stonbely, S. (2007). Racial profiling in the newsroom. *Journalism and Mass Communication Quarterly, 84*(2), 231–248.

Robertson, C. T., Selva, M., & Nielsen, R. K. (2021, March 21). *Race and leadership in the news media 2021: evidence from five markets.* Retrieved from Reuters Institute University of Oxford: https://reutersinstitute.politics.ox. ac.uk/race-and-leadership-news-media-2021-evidence-five-markets.

Royal Commission on Aboriginal Peoples. (1996). *Highlights from the Report of the Royal Commission on Aboriginal Peoples.* Retrieved July 17, 2013, from Aboriginal Affairs and Northern Development Canada, Government of Canada: http://www.aadnc-aandc.gc.ca/eng/1100100014597/11001000146 37#chp6.

RTNDA Canada. (2006). *Everyone's Story: Reflecting Canada's Diversity.* Toronto: Radio-Television News Directors Association.

Siapera, E. (2010). *Cultural diversity and global media: The mediation of difference.* Chichester: Wiley-Blackwell.

Spears, G., Seydegart, K., & Zulinov, P. (2010). *The News Balance Report: Interim Report.* Toronto, ON: Canadian Broadcasting Corporation.

Special Committee on the Participation of Visible Minorities in Canadian Society. (1984). *Equality now!* Ottawa, ON: Queen's Printer for Canada.

Tolley, E. (2016). *Framed: media coverage of race in Canadian politics.* Vancouver: UBC Press.

United States Census Bureau. (2019, July 1). *Quick Facts United States.* Retrieved from United States Census Bureau: https://www.census.gov/ quickfacts/fact/table/US/PST045219.

Wilson, C. C., Gutierrez, F., & Chao, L. (2013). *Racism, sexism, and the media: multicultural issues into the new communications age* (4th ed.). Thousand Oaks, CA: Sage.

Women in Journalism. (2020, September 16). *A week in British newsrooms.* Retrieved from Women in Journalism: https://womeninjournalism.co.uk/lack-diversity-british-newsrooms/.

Zeldes, G., & Fico, F. (2005). Race and gender: An analysis of sources and reporters in the networks' coverage of the 2000 presidential campaign. *Mass Communication & Society, 8*(4), 373–385.

Zeldes, G., Fico, F., & Diddi, A. (2007). Race and gender: An analysis of the sources and reporters in local television coverage of the 2002 Michigan gubernatorial campaign. *Mass Communication & Society, 10*(3), 345–363.

5   News Organizations Respond to the Reckoning

Introduction

As Black Lives Matter (BLM) protests gained global momentum in 2020, racialized and Indigenous journalists forced mainstream new organizations to "reckon" with a history of racist news coverage and hiring practices extending to the present. The previous chapters have described some of the responses, ranging from the *Los Angeles Times'* special edition examining its own complicity in discriminatory coverage, to layoffs of racialized staff at Global News. In many cases, concerns raised by journalists were met with initial resistance and strict adherence to ethical orthodoxy; however, some news managers and organizations accepted the concerns and the calls for change. Invariably there was a public relations component in managing the criticism and calls for reform directed at news media, as well as the range of measures different companies publicly announced to address those calls. This chapter looks at reactions and steps taken by the CBC, ABC, *The New York Times*, *The Washington Post*, *The Toronto Star*, Vice News, Gannett Co., Postmedia, BBC, *The Philadelphia Inquirer*, *The Age*, ABC (Australia), *The Minneapolis Star Tribune*, and *The Globe and Mail* and others. It catalogues and analyzes the range of responses by news media based on the issues driving calls for change and how organizations reacted, focusing on some of the more innovative approaches, especially those intended to create more space for racialized and Indigenous voices in news content and the workplace. The analysis is not intended to capture every initiative undertaken by news outlets through the racial reckoning, but to reflect the range of measures it inspired.

The Analysis: Management Resists

Under the barrage of criticism from racialized and Indigenous journalists and their allies, news organizations began to speak to the

DOI: 10.4324/9781003261544-6

accusations of discrimination directed their way, and in many cases, to take concrete action. Reaction seemed to follow a general pattern, a similar sequence of events in the days after George Floyd's murder. When news outlets were criticized from within, either for their coverage of BLM protests and systemic racism or their treatment of non-white staff, management frequently reacted with silence or denial. In all-staff emails or town halls, the organization's record on diversity and inclusion was defended, and so was the journalism, citing the importance of a range of opinions/free speech, the need for objectivity and to avoid the appearance of bias. When management's initial position drew further reproach, top executives would relent, admit mistakes had been made, promise to do better, apologize, and in cases involving content, they might have pulled stories, allowed space for counterargument, or added a correction or editor's note. In some cases, these measures were followed up with personnel measures such as leaves or suspensions, resignations, reassignments, or firings. Frequently that is where the actions by news leaders ended, but for some, the initial reckoning launched a process of dialogue and discussion leading to a range of additional long-term reforms.

The responses of mainstream news outlets to the calls for change in 2020 were prominent on their own social media platforms, and print and web pages, undoubtedly motivated by the desire to manage the public relations battle. As described in Chapter 1, there was considerable pressure mounted on the corporate world to address its records of discrimination and to join the anti-racism movement. Media accounts of the statements by news executives or senior communications staff emerged detailing their responses to the reckoning, particularly in the United States and Canada, but also in Australia and the United Kingdom. What follows is an analysis of those responses, the issues that inspired the reactions, and examples from specific media outlets. Two overarching categories emerge, one related to criticism over harmful, racist content, the other based on working conditions for Indigenous and racialized news staff.

Addressing Harmful Content

Table 5.1 provides an overview of the first category, divided into subcategories of specific harmful content, and the long-term record of producing harmful content related to Indigenous and racialized communities. The former captures instances where news organizations published material related to news-of-the-day issues and events, such as BLM protests, police violence, and systemic racism in society

Table 5.1 Responses to harmful, racist content

Issue Driving Action	Response	News Organization Examples
Specific harmful content	• Deny there's an issue, defend editorial direction	*New York Times,* Global News
	• Apologize for mistakes, editorial direction	Postmedia, Philadelphia Inquirer
	• Firings, resignations, reassignments, suspensions	*New York Times, The Age*
	• Take stories down, add editor's notes, publish critical or rebuttal content	Postmedia, *New York Times,* CBC News
	• Publish stories on news media and race	*Toronto Star, The Guardian*
Long-term record of producing harmful content	• Apologize for editorial direction	*L.A. Times,* Winnipeg Free Press, *Kansas City Star*
	• Create content describing the record of harm	*L.A. Times,* Winnipeg Free Press, *Kansas City Star*
	• Establish editorial positions dedicated to diversity and inclusion	*Toronto Star, Washington Post, San Antonio Express-News*
	• Develop space for marginalized content	*San Antonio Express-News,* Gannett, Winnipeg Free Press, *The Globe and Mail*

Source: The author.

(debates and discussions raised by the BLM movement). The latter reflects the history of inequitable, stereotypic, and sensational news coverage in mainstream news media. Table 5.1 also provides examples for each response from specific news organizations, described below. Some of these responses were referenced in Chapter 1 but are touched on again in the context of this analysis.

Specific Harmful Content

After concerns had been raised about specific content, the initial reaction by news media managers took the form of either outright denial or qualified admission that "mistakes had been made," but usually with a defense of the editorial direction. Perhaps the most high-profile example of this was the Tom Cotton "Send in the Troops" editorial in *The New York Times*. More than a thousand employees signed a letter stating that the op-ed (among other things) was "an affront to our standards for ethical and accurate reporting for the public's interest" (Smith B., 2020). While no one denied there was a problem with the piece, and the opinion section editor James Bennet resigned, publisher A.G. Sulzberger told a *Times* reporter "we're not retreating from the principles of independence and objectivity." At a virtual town hall Bennet explained his vision for the publication's editorial pages, that for "ideas and even dangerous ideas, that the right thing to do is expose them on our platform to public scrutiny and debate" (SmithB., 2020). Executives at *The Times* "thanked staff members for their public outrage" and an editor's note was added to the online version of the Cotton essay, "saying that it contained allegations that 'have not been substantiated,' its tone was 'needlessly harsh' and that it should not have been published" (Smith B., 2020). A few weeks later, *The Times* ran the Wesley Lowery editorial on objectivity and race in which he referenced the Cotton controversy at length. In the end, the range of responses at *The Times* included apologies, the addition of an editor's note, and publishing critical or rebuttal content identified in the analysis.

In the wake of the Rex Murphy column declaring Canada is not a racist country, the sequence of events was remarkably similar at the *National Post*: Employees sent an email condemning the article to management, A town hall was held, the opinion editor called publishing the piece a "fuck up" and the premise was "indefensible," an editor's note was added, and a rebuttal column by *Financial Post* journalist Vanmala Subramaniam, titled, called "Before you declare Canada is not a racist country, do your homework" (Krishnan, 2020a). Nonetheless, both Murphy and Postmedia founder Conrad Black were allowed to write subsequent columns essentially supporting Murphy's initial premise, with Black concluding "that the overwhelming majority of our countrymen is as militantly opposed to [discrimination] as I am" (Black, 2020). When asked about the columns and further backlash, the editor-in-chief was unapologetic, stating "We stand by our columnists' right to state their opinion" (Szklarski, 2020). Consistent with the data in Table 5.1, this example includes an apology, rebuttal content, and a defense of a return to the initial editorial direction. This pattern also played out with *The Philadelphia Inquirer's* "Buildings Matter, Too" column deriding BLM demonstrations, drawing the ire of news employees, and 44 racialized journalists called in "sick and tired" in a day of protest (Snyder & Romine, 2020). The executive editor resigned, *The Inquirer* apologized, and at least two first-person columns were published describing the experiences of Black journalists, one by Jenice Armstrong, the other from Solomon Jones.

When a dozen Global News staff raised concerns about a story on BLM protests in the United States, managers met with them to discuss the issues and options. The story was unpublished with an editor's note stating the story would be put back up online once it met "their editorial standards" (Krishnan, 2020b). However, the workers suggested there ought to have been more transparency around why the article was taken down, and an apology, but one of the managers is reported to have said that "There wasn't a lot of value for us to continue to show people a mistake that our organization made." This case offers response categories of removing content, adding an editor's note, and defending the editorial direction. CBC also drew heavy criticism for some of its coverage of BLM protests in New York, much of it coming from its own staff, but issued on-air apologies and corrections (CBC News, 2020a,b). When Mi'kmaw lobster fishers set traps in the fall of 2020, outside the non-Indigenous season, it was frequently described in mainstream news as an "illegal fishery," including by the CBC. In fact, the Mi'kmaq have a treaty right to harvest lobster that has been affirmed by the Supreme Court. Criticism of the coverage prompted CBC to go public with its shortcomings and interviewed APTN Mi'kmaw journalist Trina Roache on CBC Radio. Roache explained the legal framework for the Mi'kmaw fishery as well as some of the other mistakes news media were making, such as describing Mi'kmaw activities as protests (CBC News, 2020a,b).

Some Australian news media were also forced to takes steps in response to critique over the coverage of protests. *The Age* issued a correction and an apology after it suggested in a story that an activist group was planning violence with little to no corroboration (Meade, 2020). In a pattern seen in North America, *The Age* also issued a correction after an editorial incorrectly denied Australia's historical ties to slavery. The two missteps seem to have contributed to the resignation of editor Alex Lavelle, though management would not confirm that this was the case. At the BBC, frustrations around the coverage of BLM protests, famous Black people being mixed up by hosts, and the use of a racial slur by white journalists, all contributed to a heated Zoom staff meeting (White, 2020a). However, none of the issues raised drew any formal response from management, at least not related to its news coverage.

Few mainstream news organizations emerged from the racial reckoning without being criticized for their coverage of race. A number of outlets looked beyond their own reporting to examine the media's record of under- and misrepresentation. The *Toronto Star* was an example of this, featuring critical articles from academics (Callison & Young, 2020) and activists (Hudson, 2020), as well as reviews of the news narratives on the Mi'kmaw lobster fishery and BLM protests. NPR, CBC, *The New York Times*, Vice, *Huffington Post*, BBC, *The Guardian*, and *The Atlantic* were all organizations that examined news media complicity in systemic racism in this manner.

Long-Term Harmful Content

In some cases, the discussions around race and news representation extended from current reporting to the organization's discriminatory reporting in the past. Many news outlets simply avoided the topic by committing to future diversity efforts, but three publications in particular addressed the topic in fulsome ways. Management at the *Los Angeles Times* found themselves under a heavy attack from news staff for years of obfuscation on diversity issues, and under that pressure made space for a deep accounting of the newspaper's own complicity in perpetuating racism in southern California. On September 27, 2020, the *Times* published a 3,300-word editorial, titled "Our reckoning with racism." As editorial page Editor Sewell Chan explained, the piece was not just an apology, but an attempt to "to chronicle a long history: the rooting of the Times in white supremacy" including "deplorable injustices, such as supporting the wartime incarceration of Japanese Americans" or the "1981 series that described Black and Latino criminals as marauders and predators, and a 1994 endorsement for the anti-immigrant re-election campaign of Gov. Pete Wilson" (Chan, 2020). Articles examining the *Times* coverage on a variety of racial issues by LatinX, Black, and Asian journalists accompanied the "reckoning" project and were published on the front page every day during the following week. As Chan wrote in a later piece about the experience, "An apology is just the first step; real progress comes when pluralism becomes unremarkable – when diverse stories, about diverse communities, told by diverse newsrooms, are the norm" (Chan, 2020).

The *Winnipeg Free Press* offered its own admission of complicity in systemic racism in an editorial written by editor Paul Samyn. Under the headline "An apology for marginalizing people of colour; and a promise to atone for our past," the column traces a few of the more egregious examples of editorial excess, such as a column in the aftermath of the 1919 General Strike that the time had come "to clean the aliens out of this community and ship them back to their happy homes in Europe which vomited them forth a decade ago" (Samyn, 2020).

While there was little in the way of more current reckoning, the *Free Press* did take responsibility for discrimination in the present:

> The power of the press is one that can right wrongs by shining a light. And to the extent that fundamental fault lines remain in our community based on the colour of one's skin – where people of colour are not afforded the same opportunities, the same rights, the same advantages – we must concede that it's partly the fault of this newspaper.
>
> Samyn (2020)

The article noted that the *Free Press* had committed to "a goal to have a newsroom far more reflective of the community we serve" in 2019 and had recently hired "four people of color" as full-time reporters. It highlighted other perceived successes recognizing the *Free Press* as the "first major Canadian daily newspaper to issue a treaty land acknowledgment and hire an Indigenous city columnist" (Samyn, 2020). As a follow-up to the apology, Samyn mentioned the publication was launching "a major examination of race and racism in our province – a newsroom-wide initiative that will generate stories over the course of the next several months."

The Kansas City Star launched an investigation of its own racist complicity through the racial reckoning, and began with a focus group of community leaders in which Black residents said they "don't trust the mainstream newspaper... For decades the only time they saw themselves in our pages was as perpetrators or victims of crime" (Williams, 2021). The project was called "The Truth in Black and White" and began with a front-page apology from *The Star*'s president and editor, Mike Fannin. He wrote:

> Today we are telling the story of a powerful local business that has done wrong. For 140 years, it has been one of the most influential forces in shaping Kansas City and the region. And yet for much of its early history — through sins of both commission and omission — it disenfranchised, ignored and scorned generations of Black Kansas Citians. It reinforced Jim Crow laws and redlining. Decade after early decade it robbed an entire community of opportunity, dignity, justice and recognition. That business is The Kansas City Star.
>
> Fannin (2020)

The project also featured six feature stories on *The Star*'s role in a range of racial issues over the years: the focus on Black criminality, the failure to hold racist politicians to account, the invisibility of Black success stories (including Jazz legend Charlie Parker), and support for segregation.

In social media posts and letters from readers, all three publications received praise for taking these steps which were heralded by some as groundbreaking gestures of atonement. However, the *Los Angeles Times*' Sewell Chan, after hearing from a friend who had written about the civil rights movement and the press, acknowledge "that several Southern papers" had also "revisited painful pasts" (Chan, 2020). *The Jackson Sun*, in Tennessee, sought redress in 2000 by publishing a series of articles detailing "its poor and biased coverage" on civil rights while the *Lexington Herald-Leader* released "a special report" in 2004 with the frank observation, "It has come to the editor's attention that the *Herald-Leader* neglected to cover the civil rights movement. We regret the omission." In 2018, *The Montgomery (Alabama) Advertiser* acknowledged its "indifference" to the "racial terror" of the past including lynchings. Chan wrote that "these courageous projects inspired our own apology editorial" (Chan, 2020).

In some cases, measures to bring about more inclusive coverage were announced without any reference to a specific instance of inequitable reporting. Gannett, the parent company of *USA Today* and over 250 publications, is an example of this. In a coordinated corporate communications blitz, the company released the staffing demographics for all its news units, as well as accompanying editorials by senior managers at each outlet, all promising to essentially "do better." A column by the president of news at Gannett Media and publisher of *USA Today*, Maribel Perez Wadsworth, broadly alluded to a record of poor coverage but not nearly to the degree seen in *The Kansas City Star, Los Angeles Times,* or *Winnipeg Free Press*. The focus was more on the company's efforts to improve coverage with more diverse newsrooms. Nonetheless, the column contained links to similar columns by senior editors at dozens of specific Gannett publications, each describing the racial makeup of its own newsroom and reforms being introduced at the local level. The editor of *The Des Moines Register*, Carol Hunter, began her article by referencing a headline from 1988, "Clive police urge residents: Report sightings of blacks" (Hunter, 2020). She went on to explain that "Our shortcomings today are rarely as blatant as that headline, but they're harmful nonetheless. Too often, we're blinded by our own biases in how we approach stories," and pledged editors would embrace "inclusive journalism," that more would be done to develop sources in "communities of color." At *The Arizona Republic*, executive editor Greg Burton announced in his column a range of hiring initiatives aimed at more inclusive reporting, including new positions to cover "diverse communities and systemic inequities," culture and recreation with "special attention to the experiences of Latino and Indigenous communities," and "a new beat" examining race focusing on "Mexican and Central American diasporas in the United States as well as migration of African American, Asian and Indigenous people" (Burton, 2020). Gannett's campaign is further discussed below in the section looking at the lack of diversity in newsrooms.

Issues with harmful content were often linked to the newsroom and workplace culture of the employer, and not just seen as purely an editorial concern. The next section looks how news organizations responded when called out over the work environment for racialized and Indigenous journalists.

Addressing Issues in the Workplace

Table 5.2 provides an overview of the second category identified in the analysis, divided into workplace subcategories: the lack of diversity among staff, supervisors and managers, and workplace inequity and toxic culture. Each subcategory is examined below. Compared to the harmful content category, responses related to the workplace tended to be more associated with a bigger, corporate public relations strategy similar to those seen in many other industries. Whether it was the BBC, *The Washington Post*, Gannett, Corus Entertainment (parent company of Global News), or Postmedia (owner of the *National Post* and Canada's biggest newspaper chain), corporate communications departments were involved in either announcing diversity initiatives, responding to the inquiries from journalists covering the racial reckoning, or both. This was the case when news positions were created for Indigenous news staff and journalists of color, when companies signed on to industry-wide diversity and inclusion projects, when diversity officers were hired or independent diversity consultants were brought in, and when non-white staff were appointed to prominent positions. As seen in the previous section, sometimes these measures garnered space on websites and newspaper pages, opening the door to accusations that organizations were using inclusion to burnish their corporate image.

Lack of Diversity among Staff, Supervisors, and Managers

As Table 5.2 indicates, almost every mainstream news outlet responded to the racial reckoning with at least some gesture toward diversity and inclusion, but some went quite a bit further. The weight of

Table 5.2 Responses to workplace concerns

Issue Driving Action	Response	News Organization Examples
Lack of diversity among staff, supervisors, managers	• Admit more could be done, highlight successes, promise more diversity	Most news organizations
	• Release data on diverse staffing	Gannett Co., *The Globe and Mail*
	• Create new positions for racialized staff and start hiring	*Toronto Star, Minneapolis Star Tribune, San Antonio Express-News*
	• Bring in a consultant	Global News
Toxic culture	• Firings, resignations, reassignments, suspensions	ABC News, CBC News, Refinery29, *Variety*
	• Apologize for treatment of racialized and Indigenous staff	*Washington Post,* CBC, *L.A. Times*
	• Diversity and inclusion/anti-racism training	Many news organizations

Source: The author.

the racial reckoning might not have been felt anywhere more significantly than in the city where it began, Minneapolis, and one of its most important local news outlets, *The Star Tribune*. Social distancing and masking measures were still in place when three racialized members of the news team met with a senior executive to share the concerns and frustrations of racialized workers. They pointed out that "only 14 per cent of hires in 2019 were people of color, about how often journalists of color are sidelined into night shifts, about how few are promoted into leadership positions" (Miller, 2020). This meeting was followed up by others, and eventually a document outlining potential solutions. Before long, *Star Tribune* management came back with an action plan based on that document, "promising to hire an assistant managing editor focused on diversity/community, a journalist of color as a contributing columnist, and another full-time reporter dedicated to covering race and equity in Minnesota." There were other actions promised, and in the last week of September, 2020, the *Star Tribune* announced that veteran photo editor Kyndell Harkness, a Black woman, would move into the new assistant manager role. She explained her appointment with the observation that "the room is too white. When you have a homogenous room, it makes it hard to see the nuances when covering diverse communities. You need people in the room who've been there" (SmithM.L., 2020).

The *Toronto Star* also falls into the category of adding new roles for racialized staff, but its approach was unique in that it went beyond hiring and established a new avenue for communication between staff and management. According to an internal memo, the creation of an internal ombud position was intended to offer "an alternative avenue" for staff to air their concerns related to race, providing "a safe place for BIPOC journalists and all journalists to express editorial-related discrimination and bias concerns if they don't feel comfortable bringing it to their manager directly" (J-Source, 2020). Race and gender columnist Shree Paradkar was warmly welcomed into the role by management and staff, with the exception of controversial columnist Rosie DiManno, as described in Chapter 1. DiManno responded to the announcement by cursing the move in a company-wide email. The goodwill won by Torstar management with the creation of the internal ombud quickly evaporated when it failed to discipline DiManno (Goldsbie, 2020a). Nonetheless, the *Toronto Star's* innovative approach stands out as a potentially effective way to ensure safe lines of communication for Indigenous and racialized staff who want to flag issues with content or editorial decisions, but have been afraid to raise them.

Corus Entertainment, the parent company of Global News, was an example of an organization engaging a consultant to address diversity and inclusion issues in the workplace. When Global News executives and corporate communications representatives received media inquiries related to newsroom turmoil over the racial reckoning, they frequently countered that the company had hired DiversiPro to "to conduct an external independent investigation on the company's culture" (Krishnan, 2020b). In fact, Corus features a quotation on one of its web pages from an official with DiversiPro praising Corus for its "courage and foresight" when "no other media organization in Canada has had a third-party take such a deep look into the issues of equity, diversity and inclusion" (Corus, 2020). At some point, Corus began to detail its progress on its website under the heading Diversity, Equity, and Inclusion Review, triggered by the racial reckoning. The first post on the web page begins by stating that "This is an important time in our society. Conversations about anti-Black racism, and biases and barriers for people of colour and for Indigenous peoples are more open and focused on lasting change than ever before" (Corus, 2020).

Additional information posted off the company's Corporate Social Responsibility tab details some of the findings of the review as well as plans to deal with the issues identified. This includes a matrix with headings "what we learned," "what we will do," "status" (in progress, not started, completed) and comments. There are many references to "inclusion training" for staff and managers, but also performance metrics related to diversity targets, including a survey of employees to collect racial, gender, and sexual orientation data (Corus, 2020).

Attempts to quantify participation rates of racialized and Indigenous news staff are frequently hampered by organizations that refuse to participate (see Miller, 2005; News Leaders Association, 2019). During the racial reckoning, Gannett chose to embrace real transparency on the racial representation in its own newsrooms, releasing that data for its network of publications in August 2020, mentioned earlier in this chapter. In her *USA Today* editorial, Wadsworth, the head of Gannett Media, explained the release of those statistics as part of the growing recognition by the corporate world of the value in diversity and inclusion: "This has always been true, especially in journalism. How can we hope to fully understand the issues and needs of our communities if our newsrooms don't reflect the people we serve?" (Wadsworth, 2020). Wadsworth committed Gannett to "achieving gender, racial and ethnic parity by 2025" and to report on its progress but conceded "our news organization has much work to do to achieve this goal." She did not address how the lack of diversity had impacted Gannett news content in the past, but she announced that "By the end of the year, we will have created 20 national and 40 local jobs focused on social justice, disparities and inclusion to augment our coverage of race at the intersection of every critical institution."

The data on the racial composition of individual Gannett publications were accessible through links from her editorial. The implications of the statistics are not always apparent. For example, information on the *Detroit Free Press* states that 12 per cent of its staff is Black, while 21.5 per of the "community" is Black. However, in an accompanying article, the editor of the *Free Press*, Peter Bhatia, points out the analysis includes the seven counties that make up the "newspaper designated market" (Bhatia, 2020). He writes that for his own terms of reference he prefers to consider "the three-county Wayne-Oakland-Macomb area" where the Black demographic increases to 37.1 per cent, while noting the city of Detroit is "78.6% African-American." Still, Gannett shared its racial makeup publicly, and despite the public relations feel to some of the editorials, opened the door to further scrutiny in the years ahead if it does not meet its target.

In the United Kingdom, where BLM certainly inspired social debate and discussion, if less so than in the United States and Canada, the response from news organizations was muted by comparison. *The Guardian* was an exception, and like major national news groups in North America, it devoted space on its website to highlight its commitment to "diversity, equity and inclusion" (*The Guardian*, 2021). This included a "U.K. Race Action Plan," as well as reports on gender and ethnicity pay gaps in the organization. The Race Action Plan was presented to staff in September of 2020 and committed to "nurturing a more diverse pipeline of talent" through all levels of operation and to "hold ourselves to account" (*The Guardian*, 2020). The BBC drew a lot of heat over the summer of 2020 for its news coverage as BLM protests filled streets and squares across Britain. In June, it made its first big policy announcement in response, promising to invest £100 million over three years to produce "diverse and inclusive" television content, without any mention of its news operations (BBC News, 2020). In September, after media reports criticizing news programming for its lack of ethnic representation and a toxic work environment for racialized staff, the new director-general of the public broadcaster, Tim Davie, revealed his vision for the BBC. While steadfastly defending BBC's "commitment to impartiality," a nod to conservatives decrying the "political correctness" of anti-racism and anti-colonialism views, he detailed a "modern 50/20/12" approach to diversity, "50 per cent women and 50 per cent men, at least 20 per cent Black, Asian and Minority Ethnic, and at least 12 per cent Disabled" (Dams, 2020). However, the BBC's annual report for 2020 revealed its previous diversity plan, which ended that year, had failed to deliver on promises of gender parity and on its goal of 15 per cent Black, Asian, and Minority Ethnic in leadership roles (it came in at 13 per cent), though it did achieve its overall target for non-white staff at 15.9 per cent (Lawes, 2021).

Most media companies committed to some measures, whether it was a review of its hiring practices or a launch of diversity training "immediately" in the case of Postmedia (Szklarski, 2020). Media giants such as *The New York Times* and *The Washington Post* have detailed plans for improving the newsroom culture and the content it creates, including the release of workplace demographics, similar to Gannett and Corus, and a range of hiring, mentoring, and support programs aimed at retaining and promoting all under-represented groups. The comprehensive lists of initiatives are available to the public on company websites, and do give some space to accountability, as with this pull-quote on *The Times* website: "There are hiring managers who use terms like 'diversity hire' and view hiring people of color to be a hassle in getting the best" (The New York Times, 2021). In Canada, *The Globe and Mail* also announced an employment equity survey, as well as a diversity and inclusion blueprint tied to its strategic plan (*The Globe and Mail*, 2021).

The initiatives that stand out from the decades-old promises of more "multicultural training" and hiring non-white news staff are those that target hiring at the management level, in both administrative and editorial operations, and those that create new roles for racialized and Indigenous workers as columnists or specialized reporters on specific beats where marginalized voices have been under-represented. *The Globe and Mail* hired an Anishinaabe author and journalist as a columnist and investigative reporter; *The Washington Post* created a managing editor for Diversity and Inclusion, and eight reporter positions "to enhance coverage of the growing national discourse on race," including a "race in America writer" (WashPostPR, 2020); the *San Antonio Express-News* hired new "columnists of color" (Miller, 2020); Corus Entertainment created a "Head of Diversity and Inclusion" position; the *Los Angeles Times* established an "assistant managing editor for culture and talent" and appointed Angel Jennings, a Black reporter at the *Times*, into the role, "part of the media company's efforts to reform hiring practices, increase staff diversity and overhaul how it treats Black and Latino journalists and communities" (Masunaga, 2020).

Toxic Culture

This category includes a range of microaggressions referenced in previous chapters, as well as behavior both in public-facing discourse, and in the day-to-day operations of the organization. In a societal climate of social justice brought on by the death of George Floyd and BLM, resignations (voluntary or otherwise), firings, and suspensions were commonplace. In some cases, the pressure for a response was both internal and from the public. At CBC, two high profile personalities were essentially forced off the air for what amounted to deeply insensitive language. Former Conservative cabinet minister Stockwell Day stepped down as a panelist on the political program Power & Politics after comparing systemic racism to the bullying he received as a child for wearing glasses (Zimonjic, 2020). His ardent stance in asserting that Canadians are not racist was deemed unacceptable by CBC staff and the public, and he was also forced to resign from corporate board positions as well. Journalist Wendy Mesley was suspended from her show, *The Weekly*, for using the N-word in a story meeting in which issues of race were being discussed (Goldsbie, 2020b). Mesley had used the slur in a previous meeting, though no disciplinary measures were taken in that case. Both Mesley and Day apologized on social media, and Mesley has since left the CBC.

Infamous Brexit proponent and former UK Independence Party leader Nigel Farage was also forced off the air in a campaign led by coworkers at Global Media, owner of the radio station LBC, where Farage was a host. Farage had repeatedly attacked BLM activists and leaders, but staff called for his dismissal after he "compared Black Lives Matter to the Taliban" and criticized "the toppling of statues of slave owners" (White, 2020b). Global Media noted that Farage's contract was due to expire and thanked him "for the enormous contribution he has made to LBC." In Australia, Channel Nine Host Brooke Boney, a Gamilaroi woman, endured stereotypic comments targeting Indigenous residents of public housing by One Nation Senator Pauline Hanson (Eden, 2020). The conservative politician had been a regular commentator at the network but was dropped after the exchange with Boney, who later said she was left "completely heartbroken" by Hanson's remarks. Channel Nine also cut an Australian rules football commentator, Sam Newman, after pressure from employees and players. Newman called George Floyd a "piece of shit" on his podcast, prompting one Channel Nine journalist to state that he was ""ashamed this clown is employed by the same company as me" (Zhou, 2020).

Executives at a long list of organizations faced accusations of toxic behaviour and a range of disciplinary measures: *Bon Appetit*, *Variety*, *Vogue*, Refinery29, ABC News and Global News. Some apologized, some were put on administrative leave, and some resigned. Accusations of insensitive comments prompted an independent, internal investigation of Barbara Fedida at ABC News, which confirmed the accusations against her, including "that Ms. Fedida managed in a rough manner, and on occasion, used crass and inappropriate language" (Steinberg, 2020).

Despite the backlash against so-called cancel culture and political correctness, news organizations held to account by the concerns of their own staff – during a racial reckoning – had little choice but to take drastic action against prominent leaders called out for behaving badly. Apologies to employees affected were commonplace, as were hastily announced plans for diversity and inclusion training. These measures in particular could be announced as a swift response to outcries of impropriety. They were not necessarily token gestures, and many organizations followed up with substantive plans, detailed throughout this chapter. Unfortunately, in some cases, quick apologies and an online seminar on unconscious bias were where the response ended.

Conclusion

Chapter 4 described decades of diversity initiatives that focused almost exclusively on trying to staff newsrooms with people of color and Indigenous Peoples. The results were some improvements in participation rates from non-white news staff, but fuller participation was held back by issues with retention. News media failed to recognize the influence of white dominant production norms and ethics on both the news content and the workplace experience of racialized reporters. Through the racial reckoning it became clear these problems needed to be addressed if mainstream news organizations were ever going to provide accurate, authentic, and equitable coverage of Indigenous and racialized communities. While some media companies offered little in the way of responses to the calls for reforms, others did, and based on the analysis in this chapter, sought to offer solutions beyond simplistic promises to hire more diverse candidates. Notable measures included real accountability for current and past mistakes, and an acknowledgment of the news media's complicity in racial discrimination; transparency in releasing racial participation rates among newsroom staff and then tracking progress toward parity; creating space for underrepresented perspectives and hiring reporters and executives to do the work; building in additional supports for racialized and Indigenous journalists by ensuring there are non-white supervisors and managers on staff; and committing to a truly equitable newsroom and news coverage by disciplining staff who engage in toxic behavior that undermines that goal. The next chapter assesses journalism's latest pivot to diversity and inclusion and seeks to identify the measures likely to have real and long-lasting impact.

References

BBC News. (2020, June 22). *BBC commits £100m to increasing diversity on TV*. Retrieved from BBC: https://www.bbc.com/news/entertainment-arts-53135022.

Bhatia, P. (2020, August 20). *Diversity matters. And the Free Press itself must do better*. Retrieved from USA Today: https://www.usatoday.com/story/news/local/michigan/2020/08/20/detroit-free-press-staff-diversity-inclusion/5607357002/.

Black, C. (2020, June 27). *Conrad Black: Much to love about Canada, despite any imperfections.* Retrieved from National Post: https://nationalpost.com/opinion/conrad-black-much-to-love-about-canada-despite-any-imperfections.

Burton, G. (2020, August 20). *From the Republic editor: Our pledge for a newsroom that reflects our diverse community.* Retrieved from USA Today: https://www.usatoday.com/story/news/arizona-republic/2020/08/20/arizona-republic-editor-our-pledge-newsroom-reflects-our-community/5603204002/.

Callison, C., & Young, M. L. (2020). *Reckoning: journalism's limits and possibilities.* New York: Oxford University Press.

CBC News. (2020a, June 3). *@CBCNews.* Retrieved from Twitter: https://twitter.com/CBCNews/status/1268341771156717569.

CBC News. (2020b, September 18). *Mi'kmaw journalist assesses media coverage of fisheries dispute.* Retrieved from CBC News: https://www.cbc.ca/news/canada/nova-scotia/media-coverage-indigenous-issues-mi-kmaw-fishery-marshall-decision-1.5730472.

Chan, S. (2020, October 8). *To move forward on racial equity, newsrooms need to reckon with their pasts.* Retrieved from Nieman Reports: https://niemanreports.org/articles/to-move-forward-on-racial-equity-newsrooms-need-to-reckon-with-their-pasts/.

Corus. (2020, November 12). *Diversity, equity & inclusion review.* Retrieved from Corus Entertainment: https://www.corusent.com/diversity-inclusion-review/.

Dams, T. (2020, September 8). *Tim Davie makes his mark in first week as BBC Director General.* Retrieved from IBC365: https://www.ibc.org/trends/tim-davie-makes-his-mark-in-first-week-as-bbc-director-general/6593.article.

Eden, G. (2020, August 17). *Karl Stefanovic under fire after comments on media diversity report.* Retrieved from SBS News: https://www.sbs.com.au/news/the-feed/karl-stefanovic-under-fire-after-comments-on-media-diversity-report.

Fannin, M. (2020, December 20). *The truth in Black and white: An apology from The Kansas City Star.* Retrieved from The Kansas City Star: https://www.kansascity.com/news/local/article247928045.html.

Goldsbie, J. (2020a, June 9). *Wendy Mesley suspended from hosting duties after using "word that should never be used".* Retrieved from Canadaland: https://www.canadaland.com/wendy-mesley-suspended-from-the-weekly/

Goldsbie, J. (2020b, August 26). *"Degrading and aggressive": Star newsroom rises up against Rosie DiManno.* Retrieved from Canadaland: https://www.canadaland.com/toronto-star-newsroom-rises-up-against-rosie-dimanno/.

Hudson, S. (2020, June 18). *Canadian media has failed Black people.* Retrieved from Passage: https://readpassage.com/canadian-media-has-failed-black-people/.

Hunter, C. (2020, August 20). *Register editor: We're going on the record and pledging to better reflect our community in staffing and coverage.* Retrieved from USA Today: https://www.usatoday.com/story/opinion/columnists/from-the-editor/2020/08/20/des-moines-register-diversity-pledge-coverage-staffing-match-central-iowa/5598062002/.

J-Source. (2020, August 20). *Memo: Shree Paradkar named 'first internal ombud' at the Toronto Star.* Retrieved from J-Source: https://j-source.ca/memo-shree-paradkar-named-first-internal-ombud-at-the-toronto-star/.

Krishnan, M. (2020a, June 12). *Journalists At Canada's biggest conservative newspaper revolt over column denying racism.* Retrieved from Vice News: https://www.vice.com/en/article/5dz3wq/journalists-at-national-post-canadas-biggest-conservative-newspaper-revolt-over-rex-murphy-column-denying-racism.

Krishnan, M. (2020b, August 20). *In the midst of a race reckoning, Global News laid off some of its most vocal internal critics.* Retrieved September 2, 2020, from Vice News: https://www.vice.com/en/article/jgx4ek/in-the-midst-of-a-race-reckoning-global-news-laid-off-some-of-its-most-vocal-internal-critics.

Lawes, R. (2021, July 7). *BBC failing to hit diversity targets.* Retrieved from C21-Media: https://www.c21media.net/news/bbc-failing-to-hit-diversity-targets/.

Masunaga, S. (2020, September 11). *L.A. Times reporter Angel Jennings is named newsroom head of culture and talent.* Retrieved from Los Angeles Times: https://www.latimes.com/business/story/2020-09-11/angel-jennings-assistant-managing-editor-culture-talent.

Meade, A. (2020, June 14). *Journalists at the Age express alarm over increasing politicisation and loss of independence.* Retrieved from The Guardian: https://www.theguardian.com/media/2020/jun/14/journalists-at-the-age-express-alarm-over-increasing-politicisation-and-loss-of-independence.

Miller, E. (2020, September 1). *How two local newsrooms are sewing diversity into the fabric of their organizations.* Retrieved from Poynter.: https://www.poynter.org/business-work/2020/how-two-local-newsrooms-are-sewing-diversity-into-the-fabric-of-their-organizations/.

Miller, J. (2005). Who's telling the news? Racial representation among news gatherers in Canada's daily newsrooms. *International Journal of Diversity in Organizations, Communities and Nations*, 5, 1–10.

News Leaders Association. (2019, September 10). *2019 Diversity survey: Digital-only platforms drive race and gender inclusion among newsrooms in 2019 ASNE Newsroom Diversity Survey.* Retrieved December 12, 2020, from News Leaders Association: https://www.newsleaders.org/2019-diversity-survey-results

Samyn, P. (2020, July 3). *An apology for marginalizing people of colour; and a promise to atone for our past.* Retrieved from Winnipeg Free Press: https://www.winnipegfreepress.com/local/an-apology-for-marginalizing-people-of-colour-and-a-promise-to-atone-for-our-past-571623212.html.

Smith, B. (2020, June 7). *THE media equation: Inside the revolts erupting in America's big newsrooms.* Retrieved July 13, 2020, from New York Times: https://www.nytimes.com/2020/06/07/business/media/new-york-times-washington-post-protests.html.

Smith, M. L. (2020, September 30). *Star Tribune names first editor for diversity and community.* Retrieved from Star Tribune: https://www.startribune.com/star-tribune-names-first-editor-for-diversity-and-community/572581112/.

Snyder, A., & Romine, T. (2020, June 5). *Philadelphia Inquirer journalists call out sick after paper publishes the headline: 'Buildings Matter, Too'.* Retrieved from CNN: https://www.cnn.com/2020/06/05/us/philadelphia-inquirer-headline-controversy-trnd/index.html.

Steinberg, B. (2020, July 20). *ABC News executive Baebara Fedida will leave after.* Retrieved from Variety: https://variety.com/2020/tv/news/barbara-fedida-leave-abc-news-investigation-1234711571/.

Szklarski, C. (2020, July 8). *Calls grow for news outlets reporting on systemic racism to address own failures.* Retrieved from CTV News: https://www.ctvnews.ca/canada/calls-grow-for-news-outlets-reporting-on-systemic-racism-to-address-own-failures-1.5016691.

The Globe and Mail. (2021, June). *The Globe and Mail diversity, equity and inclusion report.* Retrieved from The Globe and Mail: https://static1.squarespace.com/static/59fcd1bbfe54ef4e754cb673/t/6166e292689bcd-6f4ec25165/1634132632092/Globe_diversityreport_2021.pdf.

The Guardian. (2020, September). *GNM race action plan.* Retrieved from The Guardian: https://uploads.guim.co.uk/2021/09/13/Race_action_plan.pdf.

The Guardian. (2021, April 30). *Diversity, equity and inclusion.* Retrieved from The Guardian: https://www.theguardian.com/about/2021/apr/30/diversity-equity-and-inclusion.

The New York Times. (2021, February 24). *A call to action.* Retrieved from The New York Times: https://www.nytco.com/company/diversity-and-inclusion/a-call-to-action/

Wadsworth, M. P. (2020, August 20). *Gannett news president: Diversity and inclusion are choices, not just words. Today we reaffirm our mission.* Retrieved from USA Today: https://www.usatoday.com/story/opinion/columnists/2020/08/20/gannett-releases-diversity-numbers-and-2025-pledge/3386638001/.

WashPostPR. (2020, June 18). *The Washington Post announces more than a dozen newsroom positions to be focused on race, including Managing Editor for Diversity and Inclusion.* Retrieved from The Washington Post: https://www.washingtonpost.com/pr/2020/06/18/washington-post-announces-more-than-dozen-newsroom-positions-be-focused-race-including-managing-editor-diversity-inclusion/.

White, N. (2020a, August 28). *Exclusive: BBC staff accuse corporation of being 'institutionally racist'.* Retrieved from Huffington Post UK: https://www.huffingtonpost.co.uk/amp/entry/bbc-institutionally-racist_uk_5f3f9c-78c5b697824f977779/?__twitter_impression=true&guccounter=2&guce_referrer=aHR0cHM6Ly93d3cudGhlZ3VhcmRpYW4uY29tL2NvbW1lbnRpc2ZyZWUvMjAyMC9zZXAvMDIvYmxhY2stam91cm5hbGlzdC1ltZWR.

White, N. (2020b, November 6). *Exclusive: Global Media staff demanded 'racist' Nigel Farage's removal from LBC.* Retrieved from HuffPost: https://www.huffingtonpost.co.uk/entry/nigel-farage-lbc-global-media-staff_uk_5edf9d9dc5b66a22b3803845.

Williams, M. R. (2021, January 26). *To change its future, The Kansas City Star examined its racist past.* Retrieved from Nieman Reports: https:// niemanreports.org/articles/to-change-its-future-the-kansas-city-star-examined-iots-racist-past/.

Zhou, N. (2020, June 19). *Sam Newman resigns from Channel Nine after comments about George Floyd.* Retrieved from The Guardian: https://www.theguardian.com/media/2020/jun/19/sam-newman-resigns-from-channel-nine-after-comments-about-george-floyd.

Zimonjic, P. (2020, June 3). *Stockwell Day exits CBC commentary role, corporate posts after comments about racism in Canada.* Retrieved from CBC News: https://www.cbc.ca/news/politics/stockwell-day-systemic-racism-canada-1.5597550.

6 Conclusion
Strategies That Work

Introduction

This final chapter reflects on the events of 2020, the demands for reform, the responses to those demands, and considers the range of diversity and inclusion initiatives that emerged. For decades, the battle cry for journalism's diversity advocates has been the call to hire people from outside the white, male, able-bodied, heteronormative group that has dominated the workforce. While that remains imperative to better representation in the news media, the reckoning offered the latest – and ample – evidence of why additional work needs to be taken on by news organizations. Twentieth century "just the facts" approaches to newsgathering cannot manage the increasing diversity of Western societies in the 21st century, not when presidents lie and spread misinformation, when entire segments of the public reject the science of vaccines and climate change, and when white parents march in opposition to the teaching of racist history. Based on the analysis of the racial reckoning earlier in this book, this chapter charts a path forward that includes newfound accountability, that creates space for racial, Indigenous, and marginalized groups in the news discourse, that incorporates additional supports alongside hiring, and that recognizes journalism's professional ideology and ethical foundation must move away from the objective orthodoxy of the past. These are all approaches news organizations undertook through 2020. At the time of this writing, it is too early to tell if newsgathering is becoming more authentic, more representative, and more equitable. The early reviews are mixed. However, the social climate has shifted, and social justice has been overshadowed by an emerging opposition to Critical Race Theory (CRT) and diversity and inclusion programs in schools, universities, and government institutions. It is not hard to find news media still making familiar mistakes in the coverage of race. Despite

DOI: 10.4324/9781003261544-7

a deep commitment to reform on the part of the news industry, the potential for misrepresentation of marginalized groups is a long way from being a thing of the past.

Accountability and Transparency

As described in the previous chapter, some news organizations took innovative steps to offer accountability to their employees, and to their audiences. While many companies admitted they had "made mistakes" in the past, just a handful took responsibility for discriminatory coverage that undoubtedly shaped public perception on issues ranging from immigration to Indigenous rights to crime. These efforts went beyond public relations campaigns and website testimonials of some media groups, to include editorial commentary and even news coverage on the role the outlet had played in advancing racist ideas. Chapter 5 noted the work done by the *Los Angeles Times*, *The Kansas City Star* and the *Winnipeg Free Press* to address their complicity in systemic racism. Just about everyone involved in these projects noted the importance of this work to build trust with racialized and Indigenous communities, but there were other, profound effects as well. At *The Kansas City Star*, the public praised the apology and articles related to the way Black people had been reported on in the past and called for more stories about racialized communities and the hiring of more journalists of color. At the same time, *The Star's* reporters learned of a racist past they were not fully aware of, and in the long run, changed the way they do journalism, as the publication's education writer Mará Rose Williams concluded,

> We will approach every story we write differently. We will question our intentions, use of language, placement of stories and decisions about what we cover and what we don't. Doing this project changed the way each of us does day-to-day journalism.
>
> Williams (2021)

Clearly this approach has a significant impact on the newsroom, public perception, and the historical record. It provides a "reset" on journalistic ethics, acting as a sort of "correction" for years of misreporting. As Williams observed, "The entire staff recognized this project would not stop at publication. It would be an ongoing effort involving every one of them." The white-dominated, one-sided reporting of the past was exposed, and the distortions in "the first draft of history" are replaced with truth-telling. Given the debate over the historic toll of colonialism, slavery, and racism through the racial reckoning, such accountability projects move journalism away from the objectivity dogma of the past and reinforce journalism's commitment to truth, fairness, and public service. Moreover, they force a news organization to confront its own biases and white dominance. Through the racial reckoning, racialized and Indigenous journalists frequently described the lack of understanding and knowledge white colleagues displayed when it came to the history of colonialism and exclusion. While "diversity" or "multicultural" training is a common response by employers when such ignorance is exposed, the very act of reporting on issues of racism and discrimination in these projects is clearly much more effective in educating journalists on the issues. And taking responsibility for distorted, fearful reporting of the past need not end after the first series, or be confined to issues of race. The *Los Angeles Times* followed up its initial apology and series in the fall of 2020 with an editorial on how its coverage of the transgender community had "failed," used "offensive language" and "perpetuat[ed] stereotypes" even as it reported on anti-trans violence (Ray, 2021).

As part of these accountability projects for past journalistic transgressions, news organizations also promised to be accountable for present and future reporting. This included pledges to hire more senior staff and journalists from non-white and marginalized groups, and to diversify news sources, but in a few cases, there were additional initiatives to back these pledges with transparency. Several companies announced plans to release annual demographic data on staffing, showing progress, or the lack of it, in boosting diversity among employees. Global News, BBC, the *Globe and Mail*, Gannett and *The Washington Post* are examples of this described in the previous chapter. However, some organizations are also looking at how well they incorporate different backgrounds into their content with diversity audits of their sourcing. National Public Radio (NPR) has engaged in this process, targeting national programing first and then local stations, so that all its shows and podcasts are "now engaged in source tracking" (NPR Extra, 2020). Three journalists at KQED television and radio in San Francisco wrote about their experiences with source audits, arguing that "despite our best intentions, we won't know who is in our stories until we count them" (Sung, Blakeley, & Tong, 2021). They noted some organizations have been doing this regularly, and that the findings have been "pretty bleak." Still, they advocate releasing those statistics to the public, pointing out that it "takes a lot of courage to make unflattering findings public, but it also reveals a commitment to the principles of transparency journalists seek in other institutions and a call to be better." The data is critical to assessing how well a newsroom is meeting its diversity goals. Performance is measured against "parity" measures, the "demographic benchmark" of ethno-cultural groups, gender, sexual identity or other lines of difference found in the news organization's audience (Canadian Association of Broadcasters, 2004; Zeldes, Fico, & Diddi, 2007). Gannett does this by comparing the racial makeup of its newsrooms to the communities they serve. It is important to note that these sorts of metrics are purely quantitative, and do not say much about the nature of the media representations. However, without them it is impossible to know if organizations are making any real progress on their diversity promises.

While some organizations have considered their staffing, sourcing, and audience metrics over the years, many have not, including most news media in Canada, Australia, and the United Kingdom. Making these measures available to the public strengthens the commitment to change, and the newfound transparency embraced by some companies seems to have been driven by demands of the racial reckoning. Organizations that claim they are committed to diversity, equity, and inclusion, who fail to measure their progress and to share it publicly, are much less likely to advance beyond the status quo.

Another approach that drew some discussion through the racial reckoning was the concept of ombuds and public editors. The position has its origins in Scandinavia, in the 19th century, and in news organizations it serves as the "point-person for reader complaints, as well as an inside/outside critic of newsroom choices," often publishing their independent findings for the public and the newsroom to see (Benton, 2021). Ombuds used to be more common, but as the business model for news production fell apart, those roles were frequently among the first to be cut by austerity measures. However, the former public editor of the *Toronto Star*, Kathy English, published a paper making the case for an undated vision of the ombud, especially at a time when news organizations are looking to deliver on promises of accountability and transparency.

> As today's journalists navigate a long overdue reckoning for racial equality and realignment of the largely white patriarchal structures that continue to dominate and define global media, can our "journalistic imagination" envision a greater role for a public editor? Would the public editor role be more relevant to journalism and the publics we serve if it evolved to encompass accountability for diversity and inclusion?
>
> English (2020)

In her paper, English explores the significant work of early Black American ombudsmen such as Robert Maynard, who became a leader in the "press desegregation movement" in the 1970s, and whose work lives on at the Maynard Institute, "founded to lead the fight against systemic racism in newsrooms" (English, 2020). She quotes Maynard from a speech he gave in 1978 to the American Society of Newspaper Editors: "Newsrooms have a responsibility to cure the legacy of racism."

The public editor or ombud is another tool news organization can use to ensure fair and accurate reporting on under-represented communities. The *Toronto Star*, as mentioned throughout this volume, created a separate ombud position (in addition to the public editor role) specifically to address issues of race in news content and the newsroom, a potential model for other news media. Some of the news organizations referenced in this book still have ombud/public editors: SBS and ABC in Australia, *The Guardian*, BBC, CBC, the *Globe and Mail*, NPR, and PBS (Organization of News Ombudsmen and Standards Editors, 2018). For organizations committed to diversity and inclusion, this role offers independent assessment of any editorial issue, transparency in the organizational review of the complaint, and accountability in following through on any suggested remedies.

Create Space for Under-Represented Voices

In an interview on the Canadaland podcast during the summer of 2020, Shree Paradkar, the *Toronto Star*'s newly appointed ombud, discussed her new role brokering concerns about issues of bias and racism in both news content and the workplace, before decrying mainstream Canadian media's poor track record on race. "We talk about racism because something racist happened. Racism for me, it's every sector of what we do. And racism should be a lens that we apply – all of us! – apply to every decision" (Paradkar, 2020). Race, she argued, "should not be a separate beat" where reporters call up Black people "as if just because you're black you're supposed to have all the analysis ready."

Her point, drawing on her experience as a race and gender columnist and observations of the racial reckoning, is that systemic racism is present in all aspects of society. Creating a news beat for a specific race or ethnic group comes off as another ham-handed shortcut by white managers seeking quick wins to display on the company's diversity web page. Writing about coverage of the Asian community in the *Los Angeles Times*, Teresa Watanabe suggested all groups should be well-represented in news coverage, not because they belong to a particular community: "The question isn't really how to cover Asian Americans; it is how to cover Los Angeles, because we, along with other racial and ethnic communities, are Los Angeles" (Watanabe, 2020). She talked to a former *Korean-American Times* reporter, Peter Hong, who called the idea of a "dedicated Asian American beat an outdated model that is 'so 1980s.'"

Mainstream news media fumble coverage of discrimination regularly, but their sins extend to ignoring and misrepresenting a range of marginalized groups, over-representing white, male, and heteronormative voices, and following a news agenda that conforms to dominant white audience expectations. To counter the whiteness "default," news media need to create space for non-white perspectives. After being called out through the racial reckoning, some news groups came up with more sophisticated ways to make space for non-white voices, such as hiring Indigenous and racialized columnists, especially at publications where the editorial writers were predominantly white. In the months before George Floyd's murder, the *Los Angeles Times* made Frank Shyong its first Asian American Metro columnist. Shyong believes "ethnic reporting is an intervention in the white perspective that is embedded in journalism" (Watanabe, 2020). As described in Chapter 3, ethnic reporting removes the white lens on the world, decolonizing newsgathering and creating content devoid of "stereotypes and objectification" (Knopf, 2010, p. 93). A race "beat" compartmentalizes ethnicity and cultures and sets it apart from other coverage, when all groups should be broadly represented in news content. It racializes news production, and sets the coverage of Black, LatinX, Indigenous, or Asian people as separate from white society. An ethnic media approach creates space in the news discourse, displacing over-represented white perspectives.

In the years before the death of George Floyd, two organizations featured prominently in this volume used principles of ethnic reporting and developed highly successful approaches to authentic reporting of racialized and Indigenous Peoples: The CBC and *The New York Times*. CBC Aboriginal, which has since become CBC Indigenous, was launched after the rise of Idle No More in 2013, when mainstream news media were criticized for failing to recognize the significance of the movement, while Indigenous news groups such as APTN were providing daily national coverage. CBC Indigenous is staffed almost entirely by First Nations, Inuit, and Métis journalists, and their work is featured across platforms (television, radio and digital), producing news, podcasts, and current affairs programing. Its in-depth reporting has offered authentic and contextual insight to the most important issues facing First Peoples, such as its work on Missing and Murdered Indigenous Women and Girls (J-Source, 2016). The unit pursues its own agenda, bringing an Indigenous lens to newsgathering. Stories air on network newscasts, covering a wide range of topics. At the time of this writing, headlines on the website included "Falsifying Indigenous identity a centuries-long issue, says First Nations University president," "Transgender Day of Remembrance a time to honour those lost, Winnipeg elder says," and "New exhibit in North Battleford, Sask., highlights emerging Cree artists" (CBC News, 2021). Duncan McCue, an Anishinaabe journalist and host at CBC, described the mandate of CBC Indigenous in an interview:

> The goal of CBC Indigenous is to present a wide selection of Indigenous life in this country and that doesn't always mean conflict and "us-versus-them." You will see those kinds of stories, because they exist. But you will also see "Boys with Braids", Indigenous weddings – all kinds of other important aspects of Indigenous life that is news. If non-Indigenous Canadians are going to live side-by-side with Indigenous Peoples and be good neighbors then they have to understand all the aspects of Indigenous life, not just the same tired stories we've been seeing.
>
> Indigenous Corporate Training (2016)

The 1619 Project published in *The New York Times Magazine*, which won a Pulitzer Prize, was regularly offered as an example of the kind of corrective that mainstream journalism can produce to forcefully challenge the white, colonial lens on the United States' origin story. *The Times* described it as "an ongoing initiative" launched in August of 2019, on the 400th anniversary of the first slave ship landing in Virginia, to "reframe the country's history by placing the consequences of slavery and the contributions of black Americans at the very center of our national narrative" (*The New York Times Magazine*, 2019). It began eight months earlier when Nikole Hannah-Jones pitched the ambitious idea at a story meeting, suggesting the magazine dedicate an entire issue "to examining the ways the legacy of slavery continues to shape our country" (Gyarkye, 2019). The 1619 Project featured essays, photos, and articles exploring the history of racism through slavery to the civil rights era to the present day, as well as a special section in the newspaper and a podcast series. Almost everyone involved in developing content was Black, "a nonnegotiable aspect of the project that helps underscore its thesis," according to Hannah-Jones (Gyarkye, 2019).

The work was heavily criticized, mostly from conservative politicians, including Donald Trump, but also by historians who seemed to view the project as ideological rather than an interpretation of perceived historical facts. *The Atlantic's* Adam Serwer sought to explain the controversy. He noted the tone of pessimism in the writing, observing that the content offered "a darker vision of the nation, in which Americans have made less progress than they think, and in which Black people continue to struggle indefinitely for rights they may never fully realize," questioning "the sincerity and viability of white anti-racism" (Serwer, 2019). He suggested that was an unacceptably harsh reality for many: "Americans need to believe that, as Martin Luther King Jr. said, the arc of history bends toward justice. And they are rarely kind to those who question whether it does."

In the midst of a pandemic that disproportionately affected people of color, and after a string of white killings of Black people, African American journalist Isaac Bailey cited the work of the 1619 Project as an example of the reporting that needed to be taken up by mainstream news media. He praised the willingness to present "these uncomfortable and inconvenient truths," put together by a mostly Black editorial team, and suggested "our audiences would be served well if more of us followed their lead" (Bailey, 2020). Amanda Zamora, A white and LatinX journalist, similarly praised the project and Nikole Hannah-Jones for naming "the roots of systemic injustice so that we may finally acknowledge our failures and grow through them" (Zamora, 2020).

From a theoretical perspective, both the 1619 Project and CBC Indigenous operate within a mainstream news framework that evolved out of the white dominant, exclusionary, colonial project of European settlers. However, their approaches to storytelling reverse the colonial gaze. The 1619 Project begins by challenging Eurocentric notions of America's founding fathers mythology by rejecting 1776 and the Declaration of Independence as the birth of the nation and tying the colonies' growth and development to the arrival of slaves, and free labor. Black editors, writers, and journalists centered Black historians and experts to reframe the American origins narrative by adding overlooked and under-represented racial truth.

Newsgathering teams made up of Black and Indigenous journalists decolonize the news discourse by focusing on perspectives outside white, dominant biases and assumptions. The success of these two ventures, one ongoing, one completed, offer direction for mainstream news organizations committed to authentic representation.

A New Ethical Stance

Journalism continues to face threats on many fronts, but the racial reckoning significantly challenged its enduring professional ideology and ethical standards. Ideals of truth, public service, and especially objectivity were debated at length in newsrooms and on social media. In Chapter 2, racialized and Indigenous journalists frequently linked objectivity in newsgathering to systemic racism and white supremacy. In fact, critical race scholars, quite separate from journalistic analysis, have theorized objectivity is a characteristic of white supremacy, that emotions are illogical, destructive, and irrational, and ought to be excluded from decision-making processes (Jones & Okun, 2001). Indigenous and racialized news staff described how they were branded as "having an axe to grind" and unprofessional when they challenged editorial decisions or issues with content over concerns about racism or discrimination, despite their own lived experience, being told "it's not about race" (Ansari, 2020). However, in many cases these stories actually *are* about race, yet white normative objectivity forces non-white reporters to navigate the double standard. Isaac Bailey described his experience with white co-workers "who in one breath said my writings about race were radical and irresponsible and in the next admitted they had not bothered to even study the racial history to which I was alluding and had no plans to" (Bailey, 2020). His colleagues told him he was not being objective, "no matter my depth of racial knowledge; they were 'objective,' no matter their depth of racial ignorance."

Several writers captured in the data set from Chapter 2 referenced the whiteness "default" in newsrooms and its impact on coverage of racialized and Indigenous communities. Graphic, "gritty" stories on non-white or marginalized groups go unchallenged through the editorial process because they do not offend the sensibilities of white editors or audiences. Reports on Black Lives Matter demonstrations that focus on violence and fear – and in several cases included no Black sources – are approved by white supervisors as solid, objective newsgathering. Law enforcement culpability for violence is whitewashed from headlines through contortions in passive language, where peaceful Australian protesters were "hit with capsicum [pepper] spray," or police are recorded doing "15 Not-Peaceful Things" in the United States. The word "genocide," steeped in significance, is too easily cleansed in the vetting process when it is has been used by Indigenous officials. These are all exercises in objectivity as it is still practiced on the frontlines of journalism. Perhaps it is not surprising then that addressing the uneven interpretation of ethics was among the most common reforms cited through the racial reckoning.

Objectivity – impartiality, neutrality – has been regarded with disdain for many years now. In their seminal *The Elements of Journalism*, scholars Kovach and Rosenstiel (2014) conceptualize reporting as a "system of verification" and argue that "being impartial or neutral is not a core principle of journalism" (p. 140). In addressing the work of renowned columnists and editorial writers they make the case that "news with a point of view cannot be discounted from being journalism" (p. 139). The same can be said for reporting on race or indigeneity based on lived experience. The challenge is distinguishing point of view journalism from political activism, public relations, or propaganda. Lewis Raven Wallace (2019) draws important distinctions in his book *The View From Somewhere*. He too rejects the idea of a "detached, impartial journalist" arguing instead for "facticity and nonpartisanship," that is, the pursuit of the truth "without undue influence from political parties or corporations" (p. 9). However, the experiences of Indigenous and racialized journalists through the racial reckoning, especially the clashes with management over their social media posts, demonstrate that mainstream news organizations still cling to outdated and contradictory notions of objectivity. While journalistic thought and scholarship has evolved, senior managers and editors have not kept up, it seems, and are still inclined to use objectivity as a tool to control the behaviour of news staff (Schudson, 2011, p. 75).

Among the journalists who called for changes to the ethical canon, Wesley Lowery stands out for the depth and specificity of his reforms. A term he returned to repeatedly in his *New York Times* editorial, was "moral clarity," a provision he suggested would "require editors and reporters to stop hiding behind euphemisms that obfuscate the truth" (Lowery, 2020). For Lowery, the moral clarity ideal combats the reoccurring issues in news coverage during the racial reckoning related to policing and systemic racism, and "would demand we use words that most precisely mean the thing we're trying to communicate: 'the police shot someone;'" and "would insist that politicians who traffic in racist stereotypes and tropes – however cleverly – be labeled such with clear language and unburied evidence" (Lowery, 2020). Moral clarity can be thought of in opposition to objectivity as described by the concept of moral muteness. The idea was developed by Frederick B. Bird and James A. Waters in the field of business ethics to explain the behavior of managers (Simola, 2018), whereby executives "demonstrate actions that are consistent with normative prescriptions for moral conduct but do so without the public use of moral language and without publicly acknowledging reliance on, or deference to, moral principles" (p. 2350). It occurs "when people witness unethical behavior and choose not to say anything," or when "people communicate in ways that obscure their moral beliefs and commitments" (Ethics Unwrapped, 2021). Moral muteness manifests in journalism when objectivity is used to avoid appearances of bias or partisanship, resulting in editorial decisions that ignore moral clarity. This could include parroting racist statements or obvious assertions of misinformation without the moral context. The result is language that appears impartial but undermines an even more important ethical directive, truth-telling, by distorting reality with false balance. Use of the passive voice in reporting on law enforcement is a clear and relevant example, "a man was taken into custody," or "officer involved shooting," or "George Floyd was killed." Such terminology coldly minimizes agency, accountability, and trauma. While journalism educators, professional associations, and some news organizations are working to mitigate these issues, an internet search of the phrase "officer involved shooting" produces a long list of media accounts of police firing a gun at someone, despite the issues it presents.

While the racial reckoning rekindled and highlighted objectivity's role as the de facto guiding principle in newsgathering, it is also clear from the accounts of journalists through this period that it still has a profound influence over editorial decision-making. Ethical reform has an important role to play in improving news coverage of race and difference. There are signs change has begun. Over the last several years, reporting on climate change, masking and vaccine mandates through the pandemic, and a former US president's "stolen election" fantasy have all highlighted the challenges to truth-telling when the powerful put forward false narratives but demand that "objective" news media provide equal space. Over time, mainstream news media have recognized the perils of capitulation. *The New York Times* media columnist Ben Smith explored this shift just a few weeks after George Floyd's death, observing that "the big outlets have gradually, awkwardly, given ground, using 'racist' and 'lie' more freely, especially when describing Mr. Trump's behavior" (Smith, 2020). Today's journalism, reflecting the discourse of social media, increasingly relies on more intimate, personal storytelling. The sudden growth in the popularity of podcasts is an example of this shift. For Smith, this is an "irreversible" trend, and evident in the journalists who are now "more willing to speak what they see as the truth without worrying about alienating conservatives." The racial reckoning has pushed journalism further along this path. An emerging ethical approach based on truth-telling and moral clarity, that continues to serve the public independently and free of partisan influence, will contribute to more authentic and equitable representations of Indigenous and racialized communities. As journalists continue to embrace these updated ideals, news organizations will have to accept these changes too.

The Importance of Senior Roles

Carla Murphy started working as a journalist in 2005, but by 2016 she was one of many racialized news workers who had had enough. She saw a lot of hypocrisy in newsroom diversity initiatives, understood why retention was an issue for journalists like her, and a few years later decided to create an "exit" survey of reporters leaving their chosen field. *The "Leavers" Project: former journalists of color speak about the journalism industry* is based on over 100 interviews and offers real insight as to why racialized reporters gave up on their careers. Among Murphy's most important findings: The typical "leaver" was an "African American or Black woman age 27–44" who "left journalism mid-career" and "36 per cent said they had managerial duties at that time they left journalism" (Murphy, 2020). Some of the factors that led to people quitting related to issues in the industry itself, such as low pay and layoffs, but much of it was specific to discrimination. One respondent, an African-American Black woman, described her experiences, "It was draining... constantly not being heard when I would stick up for people of color, dealing with white managers who were disconnected from the city, also dealing people in power who weren't qualified... It wasn't fun, I felt like I wasn't making a difference..." (Murphy, 2020).

The data around management roles are particularly telling. "Leaver managers" listed stress, newsroom mismanagement, and low pay as main drivers for moving on, but also cited a lack of newsroom diversity and poor advancement prospects among their biggest concerns. When asked "what it would take to retain JOC [journalist of color]" more than two-thirds included "diverse leadership" in their top three reasons (Murphy, 2020). They suggested they would have stayed if they had the same opportunities for advancement as white journalists, if they had felt supported and groomed for better roles by managers. One interviewee, a Hispanic or LatinX man, explained "If my bosses had been serious about investing in me and my professional development, whether through promotions or just cultivating my abilities, I likely would have stayed. I would have felt like my input was valued." Combined with the data from Chapter 2, the implications for diversity and inclusion initiatives are clear: racialized journalists want to work in diverse newsrooms, see the value in diverse leadership, and insist on being treated equitably with white news staff.

Murphy's findings also identify a problem in retaining diverse mid-level managers. The pipeline for diverse leaders is essentially cut off when those "manager leavers" change careers before moving into senior positions, thus leaving a void in both the mid-range and senior ranks. Some news organizations have sought to address this by creating new senior roles for racialized hires. However, such measures will only prove effective if other issues identified in the data are addressed, such as pay equity, stress, and the additional burden of diversity and inclusion initiatives, which the Chapter 2 findings show typically fall on the shoulders of racialized and Indigenous news staff. Racialized news staff at the BBC expressed the same frustrations as journalists in North America. One BBC employee told a reporter "they know many Black colleagues who have years of experience in their current positions, or are even overqualified but have been constantly unsuccessful when going for promotions and remain in junior roles on a basic wage" (White, 2020). Wilson, Gutierrez, and Chao (2013) describe how newsroom diversity creates a "surveillance system" against stereotypic and discriminatory news coverage, but in order to function effectively racialized and Indigenous journalists need the authority and support to implement editorial change. The need for diverse supervisors and managers was another one of the strongest messages delivered through the racial reckoning. News organizations that have responded with swift and targeted hiring will be well-placed to bring the required reform to newsroom culture. Those that have not are destined to endure the "status quo journalism" in which Indigenous and racialized news staff "conform to traditional journalistic norms that in most instances leaves little room for perspective or more diverse news content" (Jenkins, 2012, p. 27).

Conclusion

Newsrooms have changed. Once a landscape of typewriters, ashtrays, and white men, the workplace for journalists today reflects the progress of the last 50 years, including diversity in gender, ethnicity, ability, and sexual orientation. The pace of change was of course different in different countries, different regions, and different news organizations. The racial reckoning spurred a much faster, and more widespread embrace of diversity and inclusion than had ever been seen in the past. However, not everyone has signed on. For those who have, the racial reckoning also underscored the range of issues that need to be addressed, and also pathways to deal with them. Hiring Indigenous and racialized journalist has always been an important part of the equation, but now we know how critical it is to ensure there are leaders of color present to support and mentor young talent from underrepresented groups. We also know the way white supremacy has influenced production routines and ethical standards to the point where reporting on racialized groups has been fraught by negative and stereotypic portrayals. Racialized and Indigenous managers and reporters can form a bulwark against that type of coverage if news organizations give them both the power and the editorial space to do authentic journalism. We know admitting to past failures on reporting on race has a profound effect on newsrooms and mitigates cynicism in the community. As news organizations seek to incorporate diversity and inclusion into their corporate ethos, we know the importance of transparency and accountability to the public and to staff.

This chapter has identified the measures being taken up by news organizations that offer the best chance for success. Conversations on race have not gotten easier, but they remain inevitable. The racial reckoning proved that when they happen, change can follow.

Epilogue: The Racial Reckoning

The racial reckoning of 2020 was a powerful moment in the history of racial justice and inspired action. Through 2021, the consensus around anti-racism waned; there was pushback against the activists and the objective data that highlighted the prevalence of systemic racism in Western societies. The United Kingdom offers a case in point, where the Commission on Race and Ethnic Disparities, established by Boris Johnson in response to the Black Lives Matter protests, concluded "Britain is a model to the world of a successful multi-ethnic society" (Martin, Elsom, & Maidment, 2021). The commission reportedly "found no evidence the UK is institutionally racist – in a rejection of the common view among most activists – although there is evidence that 'overt' prejudice exists," and Britain stands as a "successful multi-ethnic and multicultural community" and as "a beacon to the rest of Europe and the world."

In the United States, the 1619 Project – an award-winning example of the work that can be done in challenging established racial narratives – started to be adapted as an educational resource in schools. However, both the project and its driving force, Nikole Hannah-Jones, were attacked by conservative politicians, and Republican legislators in five states introduced bill essentially banning the work from school curricula (Maruf, 2021). Hannah-Jones was also denied tenure when she was appointed to the Knight Chair in Race and Investigative Journalism at the University of North Carolina. The university's board of trustees "took the highly unusual step of failing to approve the journalism department's recommendation," though it did not explain why, all of which drew heavy criticism from faculty in the school of journalism (Robertson, 2021).

Hannah-Jones and 1619 also became part of Republican election campaigning against CRT and its place in the education system. The Republican candidate for governor in Virginia was narrowly elected after promising to ban CRT which he argued divides children into buckets of "privileged" versus "victims" (Cillizza, 2021). A law professor and CRT scholar from Columbia Law School described the anti-anti-racism campaign as "a cynical effort to weaponize the illiteracy and the lack of knowledge in this country generally about race, racism, and the law" (Barr, 2021). The news coverage of the issue drew some criticism on social media, where television panels of white suburban parents were asked to weigh in on their concerns, while the views of Black parents seemed under-reported (reddit, 2021). For those who marched for racial equity in 2020, these developments were undoubtedly cause for despair.

However, as some forces stepped up their resistance to social justice, there were signs of progress as well. Angela Sterritt, a CBC journalist from the Gitxsan Nation, charted the evolution she has seen in the news business in a tweet pointing out that in "2015, 'racism' was a no-no to talk about in the journalism industry. In 2017, 'colonization' was questioned in my stories. In 2019, journalists were not to give 'genocide' in Canada any weight. In 2021, all these rules are breaking" (Sterritt, 2021). A US study showed Black people made "record-breaking gains" in acquiring seats on corporate boards of S&P 500 companies, and overall, "ethnic and racial minorities accounted for 47% of all new directors, compared to 22% in the prior year" (DiNapoli, 2021).

There are still plenty of media missteps. CNN commentator Rick Santorum was let go after stating "we birthed a nation from nothing. I mean, there was nothing here. I mean, yes, we have Native Americans, but candidly there isn't much Native American culture in American culture" (Singh, 2021). *Globe and Mail* columnists John Ibbitson explained voters were becoming "resentful and untrustworthy" during the 2021 federal election in Canada in part because of "the increasing number of non-European immigrants," resulting in an editor's note being added to his piece, but not much more (Fawcett, 2021). Of course, the racial reckoning was never going to eliminate such lapses into discrimination. In fact, some observers wonder if the term "reckoning" was ever accurate given the scope of systemic racism and the backlash against those who would seek to end it. Writing in *The Washington Post*, Michelle L. Norris, suggests "unspooling" discrimination and white supremacy "will require more than just a year of so-called reckoning. It requires a full reboot and a commitment to let go of the things to which people cling, consciously or subconsciously, because going through life with advantages has its perks" (Norris, 2020). In news media, change might be coming, but there is much more work to be done. As Norris concludes, "The race toward equality isn't over. It has barely begun."

References

Ansari, S. (2020, July 3). *Canadian media is white AF — i want a mentor who has felt that.* Retrieved July 7, 2020, from refinery29.com: https://www.refinery29.com/en-ca/2020/07/9871564/mentorship-women-of-colour-media.

Bailey, I. (2020, May 29). *George Floyd, Ahmaud Arbery, and one journalist's painfully honest self-examination on racism.* Retrieved August 8, 2020, from niemanreports.org: https://niemanreports.org/articles/george-floyd-ahmaud-arbery-and-one-journalists-painfully-honest-self-examination-on-racism/.

Barr, J. (2021, October 6). *Critical race theory was the hot topic on Fox News this summer. Not so much anymore.* Retrieved from The Washington Post: https://www.washingtonpost.com/media/2021/10/06/fox-news-critical-race-theory/.

Benton, J. (2021, March 29). *From public to publics: News orgs need ombudsmen to push for more diverse representation, inside and out.* Retrieved from Nieman Lab: https://www.niemanlab.org/2021/03/from-public-to-publics-news-orgs-need-ombudsmen-to-push-for-more-diverse-representation-inside-and-out/?utm_source=Daily+Lab+email+list&utm_campaign=b8d17f2e8d-dailylabemail3&utm_medium=email&utm_term=0_d68264fd5e-b8d17f2.

Canadian Association of Broadcasters. (2004, July). *Reflecting Canadians: Best practices for cultural diversity in private television. a report by the task force for cultural diversity on television.* Retrieved September 9, 2010, from cab-acr.ca: http://www.cab-acr.ca/english/social/diversity/taskforce/report/cdtf_report_jul04.pdf.

CBC News. (2021, November 20). *CBC News indigenous.* Retrieved from CBC News: https://www.cbc.ca/news/indigenous.

Cillizza, C. (2021, November 4). *This is exactly how dumb our politics have gotten.* Retrieved from CNN Politics: https://www.cnn.com/2021/11/02/politics/critical-race-theory-virginia-governor-youngkin-mcauliffe/index.html.

DiNapoli, J. (2021, October 21). *Black Americans, women make big strides on top U.S. corporate boards - report.* Retrieved from Reuters: https://www.reuters.com/article/usa-companies-diversity-idCAKBN2H91BM.

English, K. (2020, December). *A Reckoning for relevance: redefining the role of a public editor.* Retrieved from Reuters Institute : https://reutersinstitute.politics.ox.ac.uk/sites/default/files/2021-03/RISJ_Final%20Report_Kathy_2020_FINAL.pdf.

Ethics Unwrapped. (2021). *Ethics unwrapped.* Retrieved from McCombs School of Business University of Texas: https://ethicsunwrapped.utexas.

edu/glossary/moral-muteness#:~:text=Moral%20muteness%20occurs%20 when%20people, is%20look%20the%20other%20way.

Fawcett, M. (2021, September 16). *Mainstream media blew Trump coverage — and now risks doing the same with the PPC.* Retrieved from National Observer: https://www.nationalobserver.com/2021/09/16/opinion/ mainstream-media-trump-coverage-now-risks-same-ppc.

Gyarkye, L. (2019, August 18). *How the 1619 Project came together.* Retrieved from The New York Times: https://www.nytimes.com/2019/08/18/reader-center/1619-project-slavery-jamestown.html.

Indigenous Corporate Training. (2016, May 30). *Duncan McCue: Mainstream media and reconciliation.* Retrieved from Indigenous Corporate Training: https://www.ictinc.ca/blog/duncan-mccue-mainstream-media-and-reconciliation.

Jenkins, C. D. (2012). Newsroom diversity and representations of race. In C. P. Campbell, K. M. LeDuff, C. D. Jenkins, & R. A. Brown, *Race and news: Critical perspectives* (pp. 22–42). New York: Routledge.

Jones, K., & Okun, T. (2001). *The characteristics of white supremacy culture.* Retrieved from Showing Up For Racial Justice: https://www.showingupfor-racialjustice.org/white-supremacy-culture-characteristics.html.

J-Source. (2016, September 20). *Memo: CBC Aboriginal to be renamed CBC Indigenous.* Retrieved from J-Source: https://j-source.ca/memo-cbc-aboriginal-to-be-renamed-cbc-indigenous/.

Knopf, K. (2010). "Sharing our stories with all Canadians": Decolonizing Aboriginal media and Aboriginal media politics in Canada. *American Indian Culture and Research Journal, 34*(1), 89–120.

Kovach, B., & Rosenstiel, T. (2014). *The elements of journalism: what newspeople should know and the public should expect* (3rd ed.). New York: Random House.

Lowery, W. (2020, June 23). *A Reckoning over objectivity, led by black journalists.* Retrieved July 7, 2020, from nytimes.com: https://www.nytimes.com/2020/06/23/opinion/objectivity-black-journalists-coronavirus.html.

Martin, D., Elsom, J., & Maidment, J. (2021, March 30). *Britain's race revolution: Landmark report says UK is 'a model to the world' on diversity, describes us as a 'successful multi-ethnic community'... and finds NO evidence of institutional racism.* Retrieved from Daily Mail: https://www.dailymail.co.uk/news/article-9420563/Britains-race-revolution-Landmark-report-says-UK-model-world-diversity.html.

Maruf, R. (2021, November 21). *Nikole Hannah-Jones: Anti-CRT coverage is a 'propaganda campaign'.* Retrieved from CNN Business: https://www.cnn.com/2021/11/21/media/nikole-hannah-jones-1619-project-reliable-sources/index.html.

Murphy, C. (2020, August 26). *Introducing 'Leavers': results from a survey of 101 former journalists of color.* Retrieved from Source: https://source.open-news.org/articles/introducing-leavers-results-survey/.

Norris, M. L. (2020, December 18). *Opinion: Don't call it a racial reckoning. The race toward equality has barely begun.* Retrieved from The Washington Post:

https://www.washingtonpost.com/opinions/dont-call-it-a-racial-reckoning-the-race-toward-equality-has-barely-begun/2020/12/18/90b65eba-414e-11eb-8bc0-ae155bee4aff_story.html.

NPR Extra. (2020, September 18). *Diversity, equity, and inclusion is not a project: It is our work.* Retrieved from NPR: https://www.npr.org/sections/npr-extra/2020/09/18/914455001/diversity-equity-and-inclusion-is-not-a-project-it-is-our-work.

Organization of News Ombudsmen and Standards Editors. (2018). *ONO Members around the world.* Retrieved from Organization of News Ombudsmen and Standards Editors: https://www.newsombudsmen.org/regular-members/.

Paradkar, S. (2020, August 30). *Ep. 339- Shree Paradkar.* Retrieved from Canadaland: https://omny.fm/shows/cndlnd/ep-339-shree-paradkar.

Ray, J. (2021, July 8). *Column: Past coverage failed the transgender community. It's important to recognize it.* Retrieved from Los Angeles Times: https://www.latimes.com/california/newsletter/2021-07-08/gwen-araujo-transgender-essential-california.

reddit. (2021, July 15). *Panel of white Karens decide that CRT is bad for kids.* Retrieved from reddit: https://www.reddit.com/r/WorcesterMA/comments/okxtyl/panel_of_white_karens_decide_that_crt_is_bad_for/.

Robertson, K. (2021, May 19). *Nikole Hannah-Jones denied tenure at University of North Carolina.* Retrieved from The New York Times: https://www.nytimes.com/2021/05/19/business/media/nikole-hannah-jones-unc.html.

Schudson, M. (2011). *The Sociology of News* (2nd ed.). New York: WW Norton & Company.

Serwer, A. (2019, December 23). *The fight over the 1619 Project is not about the facts.* Retrieved from The Atlantic: https://www.theatlantic.com/ideas/archive/2019/12/historians-clash-1619-project/604093/.

Simola, S. K. (2018). Moral Muteness. In R. W. Kolb (Ed.), *The SAGE encyclopedia of business ethics and society* (pp. 2350–2352). Thousand Oaks, CA: Sage.

Singh, K. (2021, May 23). *CNN drops former senator Rick Santorum after remarks on Native American culture.* Retrieved from Reuters: https://www.reuters.com/world/us/cnn-drops-former-senator-rick-santorum-after-remarks-native-american-culture-2021-05-23/

Smith, B. (2020, June 7). *The media equation: inside the revolts erupting in America's big newsrooms.* Retrieved July 13, 2020, from nytimes.com: https://www.nytimes.com/2020/06/07/business/media/new-york-times-washington-post-protests.html.

Sterritt, A. (2021, June 28). *@AngelaSterritt.* Retrieved from Twitter: https://twitter.com/AngelaSterritt/status/1409732042124787712.

Sung, K., Blakeley, J., & Tong, V. (2021, March 5). *Want to know if your news organization reflects your community? Do a source audit. Here's how.* Retrieved from Nieman Lab: https://www.niemanlab.org/2021/03/want-to-know-if-your-news-organization-reflects-your-community-do-a-source-audit-heres-how/?utm_source=Daily+Lab+email+list&utm_

campaign=98f5d49f3b-dailylabemail3&utm_medium=email&utm_term=0_d68264fd5e-98f5d49f3b-39615623.

The New York Times Magazine. (2019, August 14). *The 1619 Project.* Retrieved from The New York Times: https://www.nytimes.com/interactive/2019/08/14/magazine/1619-america-slavery.html.

Wallace, L. R. (2019). *The view from somewhere: Undoing the myth of journalistic objectivity.* Chicago: The University of Chicago Press.

Watanabe, T. (2020, September 27). *How do you cover a group as diverse as Asian Americans in Southern California?* Retrieved from Los Angeles Times: https://www.latimes.com/opinion/story/2020-09-27/los-angeles-times-asian-american-coverage.

White, N. (2020, August 28). *Exclusive: BBC staff accuse corporation of being 'institutionally racist'.* Retrieved from Huffington Post UK: https://www.huffingtonpost.co.uk/amp/entry/bbc-institutionally-racist_uk_5f3f9c78c5b697824f977779/?__twitter_impression=true&guccounter=2&guce_referrer=aHR0cHM6Ly93d3cudGhlZ3VhcmRpYW4uY29tL2NvbWllbnRpcc2ZyZWUvMjAyMC9zZXAvMDIvYmxhY2stamstc5hbGdlbRpc2llbZWR.

Williams, M. R. (2021, January 26). *To change its future, The Kansas City Star examined its racist past.* Retrieved from Nieman Reports: https://niemanreports.org/articles/to-change-its-future-the-kansas-city-star-examined-iots-racist-past/.

Wilson, C. C., Gutierrez, F., & Chao, L. (2013). *Racism, sexism, and the media: Multicultural issues into the new communications age* (4th ed.). Thousand Oaks, CA: Sage.

Zamora, A. (2020, June 26). *Overcoming systemic racism begins in our own newsrooms.* Retrieved from Poynter: https://www.poynter.org/ethics-trust/2020/overcoming-systemic-racism-begins-in-our-own-newsrooms/.

Zeldes, G., Fico, F., & Diddi, A. (2007). Race and gender: An analysis of the sources and reporters in local television coverage of the 2002 Michigan gubernatorial campaign. *Mass Communication & Society, 10*(3), 345–363.

Index

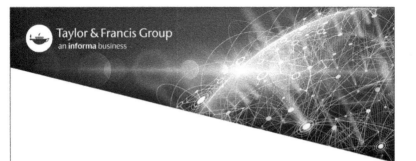

www.ingramcontent.com/pod-product-compliance
Ingram Content Group UK Ltd.
Pitfield, Milton Keynes, MK11 3LW, UK
UKHW020418010325
455677UK00029B/933